Romanticism and Education

Also available from Continuum

Philosophy of Education, Richard Pring

Theory of Education, David Turner

Romanticism and Education

Love, Heroism and Imagination in Pedagogy

David Halpin

continuum

Continuum International Publishing Group
The Tower Building
11 York Road
SE1 7NX

80 Maiden Lane, Suite 704
New York, NY 10038

www.continuumbooks.com

British Library Cataloguing-in-Publication Data
A catalogue record for this book is available from the British Library.

ISBN: 0-8264-8472-7 (hardcover)

Library of Congress Cataloging-in-Publication Data
A catalog record for this book is available from the Library of Congress.

Typeset by BookEns Ltd, Royston, Herts.
Printed and bound in Great Britain by Biddles Ltd, King's Lynn, Norfolk

For Chloe Halpin and Jacob Halpin

If I have included visibility in my list of values to be saved, it is to give warning of the danger we run in losing a basic human faculty: the power of bringing visions into focus with our eyes shut ... I have in mind some possible pedagogy of the imagination that would accustom us to control our own inner vision without suffocating it or letting it fall ...

(Italo Calvino)

Contents

Preface and Acknowledgements   1

1 Progressive Education and Romantic Energy   9
2 Romantic Images of Childhood: From Innocence to
   Transcendence   31
3 An Education in Nature and Dissent: The Romantics
   at School   51
4 Education and Romantic Love: Passion and Gusto in
   Pedagogy   71
5 Heroizing Pedagogy and School Management   91
6 Pedagogy and the Romantic Imagination   105
7 Romantic Intellectualism and Persuasive Eloquence:
   Hazlitt and the Art of Educational Criticism   129
Conclusion   145

References   151
Index   159

Preface and Acknowledgements

Drawing mainly on the literary and intellectual contributions of four nineteenth-century English writers – William Hazlitt, William Wordsworth, Samuel Taylor Coleridge and William Blake – this book seeks to recapture on behalf of education some of the chief features of Romantic sensibility, notably the high value it places on childhood, love, heroism, criticism and imagination, explaining why each has important implications for teaching and learning in today's schools.

Like the process of education, Romanticism is the mood in which we feel we are or could become greater than we know. As such, because it is an exalting of the imagination, it is a necessary condition for being hopeful about education; indeed, on some occasions, it may even be regarded in that context and others as a special case of the utopian impulse.

While Romanticism ultimately belongs to no period, there are times when Romantic thoughts, feelings and understandings are more likely. One such period included the years following the French Revolution. For reasons that we associate with the sort of political hope roused by that extraordinary uprising, the spirit of the age in England seems for 40 years after 1789 to have been especially favourable to Romantic outpourings of the imagination.

Largely the product of that spirit, it was also a period of sustained educational debate, giving rise to government plans to inaugurate a national system of state elementary schooling. It was an age, too, when particularly important ideas about education first gained an initial foothold, becoming so influential down the years subsequently that they are generally taken for granted by teachers and educators today. These include, for example, ideas about the importance of imaginative experience in teaching and learning; and ideas about the high status which should be conferred on children and the significance the early years have for their later intellectual and personal development.

The fact that such notions are nowadays mostly assumed by teachers does not of course mean that they any longer appreciate fully, or slightly, their Romantic pedigrees, least of all the significance which individual Romantic writers meant them to have for classroom practice. I suspect few educators are able to recall, for example, that Wordsworth was an early and fierce critic of teaching methods that eschewed imaginative engagement in favour of transmitting facts. In Book 5 of *The Prelude* he pours scorn on such methods, accusing those who use them of creating a 'dwarf man' of the child, who is 'fenced around, nay armed, for ought we know'. Even fewer will know that it was Coleridge, at the start of his *Biographia Literaria*, who similarly attacked the 'improved pedagogy' of his times, accusing it of communicating too much inert knowledge. What is also less appreciated is the depth of both Coleridge's and Wordsworth's commitment to the cause of popular education, which each saw as being as much about providing intellectual enlightenment for the 'lower orders' as offering them instruction in how to read and write (Connell 2001, pp. 126–7).

While it would be unfair of me to apply Wordsworth's and Coleridge's criticisms to the work of schools today, inasmuch as many teachers currently use pedagogical methods that promote learning outcomes of which they would each approve, the culture of modern schooling still places enormous emphasis on 'giving instruction', 'remembering facts' and 'teaching to the test' – approaches which I consider ultimately antithetical to promoting genuine learning. This suggests to me that there is remedial merit in restoring fully to teachers' critical consciousness some of the progressive ideals, values and beliefs of Romanticism which still interpenetrate unconsciously their thinking about teaching and learning, but not in ways that sufficiently and directly influence for the better what they actually do in the classroom.

Romantic progressivism's failure to influence the current work of teachers, however, is only a relatively recent occurrence. From the late 1950s onwards, the climate of opinion in this country about education and a host of other socially related matters became steadily very Romantic, particularly as the 1960s and 70s wore on. In the 1980s and subsequent decades this mood was supplanted by sets of attitudes about teachers' work, each often reinforced by government mandate, which reintroduced more 'traditional' – non-Romantic – approaches to pedagogy, requiring schools to manage their affairs much more along 'business' and corporate lines.

The result is that schooling nowadays in England, compared with when I first became a secondary school teacher in 1970, is more utilitarian than imaginative; more managerial than collegial; more individualist than communitarian; and more competitive than cooperative. Thus, despite what education ministers and their apologists say, England's education service at the start of the twenty-first century has not undergone modernization in any significant way. Rather, it is, in some of its most important features, one that would be recognizable to a nineteenth-century teacher – a service in which externally imposed targets and associated forms of performance management predominate, each designed to accommodate the demands of assessment rather than to promote learning for its own sake, leading to the reassertion of teaching approaches that stress the transmission of largely prescribed subject matter and instruction in the 'basic skills'. Although far more sophisticated technically, there is something similar here to the spirit and practice of the discredited monitorial and payment-by-results systems so favoured by many educational reformers over 150 years ago.

The days are long past when a teacher could say without fear of mockery that one of her intentions in the classroom is to enable young people 'to lose themselves' in learning, to feel a sense of Romantic abandonment as they become caught up in the process of engaging with new ideas, notions and experiences. Today, school curricula are not constructed to facilitate such wonderfully distracted states, and teachers are rarely publicly invited to encourage them. Instead, curricula are devised and prescribed to be delivered and digested, akin to ordering in and consuming a pizza. This is all the wrong way round. And Romanticism helps to tell us why.

In particular, Romanticism reminds today's teachers of where many of the central organizing ideas of their unconscious, as opposed to imposed, pedagogic philosophies, come from – ideas they have at the back of their minds about childhood and its special salience; about the nature of the creative imagination and schooling's role in promoting it; and about the need to treat pupils with due care and with full attention to their status as persons – but which they have largely ceased to be aware of consciously in the course of having to implement, sometimes against their better professional judgement, the welter of recent school reforms which stress an altogether different educational prospectus.

Restoring these and other Romantic themes to teachers' collective memories, I will argue, represents one means for them to re-inherit key, but currently repressed, aspects of their professional ancestry, enabling them to make better sense of their pedagogical identities, carrying with it the chance that they might then increasingly readmit progressive ideas and practices into their classroom work, while challenging those in authority who insist they do the exact opposite. As Friedenberg reminds us, Romanticism's view about the centrality of love and the life of the imagination provides a basis upon which to oppose educational processes 'by which schooling systematically alienates pupils from their own experience, and represses, ignores or reinterprets that experience in terms compatible with conventional social demands' (Friedenberg 1990, p. 177). While such a stimulus is neither a sufficient nor a necessary condition for promoting progressive change in education, the assumption I make in writing this book is that teachers are more likely to initiate such reform when they are more critically conscious of the Romantic ideas which silently stand behind their best professional intentions. Of course, many teachers presently are engaged in such reform and related innovative progressive pedagogical practice, and thus do not need me to either remind or inform them about what is required at the current juncture to oppose official expectations of what they should be doing in their classrooms. For such teachers, this book, I hope, will provide additional philosophical support for such practice, as well as fortification that it is along genuinely educational lines.

Indeed, one of the consequences for me of undertaking the research necessary to develop this book's arguments has been an increased personal awareness of how far my own pedagogic philosophy, as practised in particular during my formative professional years as a teacher – specifically between 1970 and 1975 – was itself unconsciously Romantic.

A story from that period, concerning Tony Harris, one of my former pupils, and myself, is instructive.

Tony was a member of my social and economic history class which I taught in a secondary comprehensive school in Bristol in the early 1970s. He was very difficult to motivate and caused no end of trouble on and off campus. To compound matters, he was a selective truant – that is, the sort that constructs their own personal timetable by attending school most days, but only turning up to those lessons which they want to. Mine happened to be one of Tony's, but I only discovered why after he left. Week in, week out, Tony would appear at my classroom door, slouch in and spend most of the lesson wandering around and making a general nuisance of himself. I tried every trick in the book to get him interested in the 'Spinning Jenny', the workings of an eighteenth-century lock, Stephenson's *Rocket*, and the rest. But it was useless, and I got nowhere, making things worse by my persistence. Rather than rethink what I was teaching, I simply carried on with the syllabus regardless, trying ever more imaginative ways to keep Tony and the rest of the class engaged with its topics, sometimes just busy and occupied with them. The course ended and Tony opted to leave school and get a job, and without the benefit of an examination pass in my subject. The school had this quaint routine for its leavers whereby they were not allowed finally to depart until they had seen all their teachers, said their goodbyes, and returned all borrowed books and other things. Tony turned up at my classroom to see me and get signed off. He collected my signature and listened attentively enough to my brief homily about the exigencies of the world of work that he was about to join. However, before finally taking his leave, Tony turned on his heels in the doorway and said, 'Do you know, Mr Halpin, in all your lessons, you never taught me a single thing.' While that did not come as too much of a surprise to me, I was still taken aback by Tony's effrontery. 'Well, why did you turn up each week, then?', I retorted. Without pausing for thought, Tony crisply replied, 'I just wanted to see if you would give up.'

I did not give up, partly because a form of heroically inscribed pride would not allow me to, but also and chiefly, because I genuinely wanted Tony to succeed educationally, even if he didn't care one way or another. To that extent, I was more concerned about the level and nature of his historical understanding than he was, embodying on his behalf an optimism of the will about learning some history, even though what I was teaching him about it was not sufficiently linked by me to his experience. Also, being entirely ignorant at the time of the sociology of school knowledge, I mistakenly thought that the syllabus I had been given required no justification, and that my ability to teach it well therefore depended entirely on personal verve and enthusiasm.

Mine was not on that occasion an explicitly Romantic kind of pedagogy. Even so, there were some undercurrents of Romanticism at work within it. The pity was that I did not appreciate this sufficiently at the time, with the result that I failed to make successfully the transition from being educationally earnest about what I was doing to being authentically progressive in my learning intentions. If I had known then what I now know about the Romantic impulse and its links with innovative educational practice then maybe I would have, which of course is largely my motivation in writing this book for today's teachers to read and hopefully learn from and be inspired by.

For example, my *heroism* (a Romantic notion discussed in Chapter 5, where I delineate a positive conception of the heroic in teaching, curriculum design and school leadership) might have been less charismatically and more charitably configured; while my *imagination* (another Romantic idea, which is given full treatment in Chapter 6), similarly, might have been less focused on finding clever ways of transmitting extant knowledge and more on identifying subtle approaches to co-constructing it with Tony and his classmates. Equally, my duty of care (which relates to Romanticism's championing of *love*, a theme taken up in Chapter 4), might have allowed me to develop a better appreciation of the 'nuisance value' of Tony's unwanted classroom behaviour, which I now realize may have been a form of positive attention-seeking, designed to test my reliability and loyalty. As Adam Phillips says, 'a nuisance, if we can do something with it, gives us something to be going on with' (Phillips 2006, p. 191). My lack of an explicit Romantic sensibility as a teacher in the 1970s partly prevented me from comprehending this, thus leading me to overlook an important educational opportunity. With the benefit of hindsight, based upon the experience of writing this book, I would like to think I would not make the same mistake if I had my time all over again.

One mistake I won't make now is to fail to acknowledge with gratitude the various kinds of help I have enjoyed in the course of developing the arguments which follow. First of all, I have benefited enormously from the numerous publications listed in the references at the end, including in particular the primary source material contained in some of the published writings of William Hazlitt and the Romantic poets, from which I quote extensively in places.[1] Citing such sources, of course, raises a significant methodological issue for some people – namely, how far is it reasonable to rely upon the meanings I ascribe to them in the course of illustrating or supporting a point of view of my own? The answer to this question is straightforward enough: readers can check the citation and judge for themselves, for I do not claim for a second that I have a unique understanding of what any of them means. But then I do not think that any of my sources have one essential and therefore primary meaning. Being open, and thus writerly, texts, like my own here, they are capable of being interpreted in a variety of ways.

I could not have written this book without the direct help offered by the Institute of Education, University of London, where I currently teach and research. It is an exceptional learning environment, providing excellent library facilities and inexhaustible opportunities for intellectual discussion. I drew liberally on each in the period 2004–6, during which time I pulled most of the text of this book together. Many of the book's arguments were first aired at local seminars and other similar events, and I am grateful to those colleagues and students who took the trouble either at the time or afterwards to provide oral or written feedback on what I said.

I am also grateful to the Institute for the time it gave me away from my normal teaching and administrative duties to complete the book's manuscript as part of its generous study leave programme, from which I benefited for two short periods during 2004 and 2005. In expressing my thanks at this point, I am reminded of the importance of such leave by a recent exposure to Bertolt Brecht's great play *The Life of Galileo*, during which, early on, the main protagonist is heard to complain to the Procurator of the University of Padua that he has not nearly enough time to pursue his research, only to have his pleas for more time abruptly rejected. That was certainly not my experience at the Institute.)

Various other individuals also helped me directly, to whom I also offer sincere thanks. These include Alan Day, who read every chapter in draft form, offering perceptive commentary on the coherence of my arguments and the manner of their written expression, and Barbara Baber, Claudia Lapping, Alex Moore, Costanza Preti, Lesley Saunders, Christopher Storr, Michael Strain and James Wetz, who in different ways engaged thoughtfully and helpfully with particular chapters. They also informed me of those parts of my analysis which had provoked in them positive reflection, which I naturally found encouraging, particularly during those times when I doubted the importance of what I was doing and my ability to do it.

I am grateful as well to the editors of two academic journals for permission to rework previously published articles: 'Education, criticism and the creative imagination: the legacy of William Hazlitt' (*London Review of Education*, 2. 1 March 2004: 17–33) and 'Why a Romantic conception of education matters' (*Oxford Review of Education*, 32. 3 July 2006: 325–45).

Finally, I owe a debt of gratitude to the staff at Continuum who have done so much to support my work, especially Anthony Haynes (who first commissioned the book), Alexandra Webster, Anya Wilson, Joanna Taylor and Kirsty Schaper.

None of these people, of course, is responsible in any way for the arguments I will now go on to outline and discuss. On the contrary, the analysis which follows is not just my own work, as commonly understood, but also, in significant parts, autobiographically inflected work, to the degree that it arises out of a range of personal–professional matters to do chiefly with what pedagogical aims I ought to espouse as a public educator and how I should translate these into my work with students, both in school and university settings – matters about which I have struggled academically and practically over many years. The famous sociologist C. Wright Mills once observed that 'no social study that does not come back to the problems of biography ... has completed its intellectual journey' (1959, p. 6). Although mine is not completed, it is certainly moving in that direction. My hope is that the course I outline here, or one like it, is one other people might wish to embark upon as well.

Note

1 When quoting from Romantics, I have used six main sources. For Wordsworth: Gill 1984; for Coleridge: Richards 1978; for Blake: Bronowski 1958; for Hazlitt: Wu 1998 and Howe 1928–32; and for other poets: Wordsworth and Wordsworth 2003.

1

Progressive Education and Romantic Energy

Romance is the vividness, the ferment, the excitement without which learning is barren. One may learn material and ideas, but if they are unleavened by Romance they will remain inert.

(Kieran Egan)

Re-inheriting Romanticism

Any education worthy of the name is progressive. To be educated, or to undergo an experience that is educational, always represents a form of advancement, a progression, escalation sometimes, of a person's knowledge and understanding – of themselves, of other people and of things in general.

Some educational experiences, even so, are more progressive than others, to the degree that they increase significantly the limits of what a person knows in fresh and exciting ways, and to the extent also that they stress rather than underplay or neglect particular aspects of the processes of teaching and learning. Thus a curriculum specification that only uses and emphasizes subject matter sanctioned by historic precedent, neglecting to anticipate and seek for something new and unusual – which delights in just what presently is to hand rather than looking for what may be – is not progressive but rather conservative, and maybe regressive too.

So also are modes of pedagogy which privilege teaching instead of learning – that emphasize teacher-initiated rather than pupil-directed enquiry, placing most weight on memory and bookwork and whole-class instruction and subject-based study, constructing the pupil as a near-empty vessel to be filled by pre-established, prescribed notions and facts. Progressive pedagogy, which this book is about, by contrast assumes and promotes a less passive and more active role for the student who is viewed, with the teacher, as a co-constructor of curriculum knowledge.

The progressive philosophy of schooling outlined here, while always child-centred and learning-focused, never ignores the importance of good teaching. But, in developing a framework of ideas about the sort of teaching most likely to promote effective learning, this book is consistently suspicious of certain educational orthodoxies, particularly those which lay too much emphasis on the authority of the teacher and the transmission of subject knowledge at the expense of learning how to renew or create it.

Equally, this book is uncomfortable with antiquated educational sentiments which see schooling as one means of disciplining young people, instilling in them particular 'basic skills' which are judged necessary to ensure that they function as acceptable and useful members of society. Such attitudes, which often are defended by appeal to tradition rather than reason (see Halpin and Moore 2000), are regarded as the chief bulwark against a genuinely progressive education of the kind needed in today's rapidly changing, uncertain and sometimes alienating world – a comprehensive education for life that helps young people both to accommodate and to take control of the multifarious, often competing, demands society increasingly makes upon them as they progress into full adulthood, which include handling intelligently the seductive lure of its fast-moving culture of celebrity and consumption and identifying an acceptable ideology of social hope, enabling them to enjoy lives that are as much about being as having.

Five ideas – each possessing distinctive *Romantic* roots – make up this book's progressive educational framework: *childhood, heroism, love, imagination* and *criticism*. Although they are dealt with in separate chapters, and in that order, these ideas overlap and criss-cross: being critical requires courage and imagination; being a virtuous hero frequently entails possessing a love of life and humanity, more often than not based upon unusual and ingenious insight and technique; and a particular conception of what it means to be a child is instantiated in any version of progressive teaching and learning, which assumes views about the passions, creativity, heroism and critical awareness.

While I hope these links are clearly manifest in what follows, what really matters at this point is to understand my overall purpose in seeking to make them, which is to demonstrate that particular elements of progressive education – notably ones that stress enlightened conceptions of the imagination and its creative development – have *Romantic* associations and ancestries which have either been obscured in recent times or lost sight of altogether, and whose consequent foreclosure helps to frustrate consideration of progressive ways of thinking about the practice of education. By recovering, re-inheriting and re-engaging with the Romantic ancestry of progressive education, it is my hope that those who read this book – teachers, in particular – will be encouraged to assess or reassess its relevance for their work, leading possibly to a new or renewed commitment to the ideals of a particular sort of child-centred and learning-focused pedagogy.

Studying education Romantically

My conception of the Romantic in this book carries an upper- and not a lower-case initial letter, suggesting a particular cultural entity or form of aesthetic sensibility, rather than a loosely applied adjective as might ordinarily be associated with the rhyming couplets found in Valentine cards or the plots and characters of a Mills and Boon fiction (on this literary genre, see Jay Dixon's [1999] fascinating study). Such contemporary commonplace conceptions of romance have their roots in the vernacular chivalric poems and tales that emerged in twelfth-century France in which is portrayed a marvellous quest for either love or adventure (Fuchs 2004). Although there are links between these romances and the Romantic ideas explored in this book – for example, each feature superior heroes and a positively nostalgic purchase on certain aspects of the past – they are not ones which directly influence its arguments.

Instead, Romanticism here is interpreted through an appreciation of the educational implications of certain of the literary and intellectual outpourings of a small and highly select group of English aesthetes and intellectuals – mostly poets – whose publications in the late eighteenth and early nineteenth centuries (specifically between 1785 and 1832) inaugurated a distinctive movement of ideas about the power of the imagination and the need for spontaneity in thought and action. Included here are the prose writings of the political journalist, critic and one-time painter William Hazlitt and the poetry of the so-called 'Big Six' English poets – William Wordsworth, Samuel Taylor Coleridge, George Gordon Byron, Percy Bysshe Shelley, John Keats and William Blake. In this book, Hazlitt, Wordsworth, Coleridge and Blake feature most often, with Shelley, Keats and Byron mentioned largely in passing.

Had my purpose been to write a study specifically about Romanticism (which, as I explain later, it wasn't), the inclusion of such a narrow selection of Romantic writers could not be easily excused. The fact that the writers listed here are all English *men* would not go unnoticed either, for I am aware that the masculine gendering of Romanticism is the subject of an extensive critical literature (see, for example, Mellor 1988 and 1993; Fulford 1999; Hofkosh 1998; Ross 1989). While this literature sometimes has less to do with revising radically the characteristics said to be definitive of

Romanticism, as with extending the names of the people said to represent it so as to include more women, there are occasions when it raises crucial issues about what quintessentially it means to be a Romantic.

Being products of a period in English history that accorded few rights to women, it is not surprising to find patriarchal attitudes reflected in the work of the male writers highlighted in this book. Wordsworth's conception of Nature, for example, has been criticized for being insufficiently feminine, while Coleridge and Shelley have been interpreted as advocating a version of love that privileges too much the man's perspective at the expense of the woman's. In addition, the marital lives of individual Romantics – Hazlitt's in particular, and Coleridge's to some extent also – have been exposed to reveal behaviour on their part which, judged by today's standards, does not easily escape the accusation of being crudely sexist.

Nor can I sidestep simply the objection that some of the qualities I most admire in Romantic sensibility – ones to do with heroism, energy, controversy and passion – each have a strong masculine resonance which underemphasizes, excludes even, those traditionally feminine attributes such as caring, empathy and compassion. By crafting my position in such a way, it is haunted by what it excludes (see Phillips 2006, pp. 43 and 53) – and because my position is ultimately a fiercely argued one, the mildly sexist ghost that bestrides it is all the more striking.

Accordingly, I recognize as a limitation the fact that this book marginalizes through exclusion all the great female British Romantic poets and writers of the eighteenth and nineteenth centuries (for example, Charlotte Smith, Caroline Norton and Mary Robinson). As a result, my conception of the Romantic is arguably insufficiently feminist, though I do not think that this limitation renders my overall argument redundant.

In any event, where writing of this sort is concerned, it simply is not possible to cover every angle of every issue with equal effect. Indeed, in a work of this limited scale, I had to draw a boundary somewhere, and my preference was to do this in such a way as to encompass those individuals about whom I knew the most and whose work had had the greatest impact on my thinking. I also concluded early on that adding certain women's names to my list of preferred authors would not alter substantially the kind of argument I wanted to develop, though I concede they would have enriched it by pointing up Romantic qualities which my featured writers either downplay or ignore. The challenge therefore is ultimately to judge my analysis by what it includes rather than by what it excludes.

But this is all, in the long run, beside the point, because my aim was never to produce a book about Romanticism *per se*, but rather to write one *about education*, in which aspects of the Romantic oeuvre and particular features of Romantic sensibility are used to illustrate and explicate arguments about effective teaching and learning. This is not a book for scholars of English literature looking for new critical insights into the works of particular Romantic poets. But students of education studies, who are searching for new evaluative and inspirational ideas about teaching and learning, are invited to read on and stay the course. For this is very much a book for them, even though, for their benefit, and particularly for those among them unfamiliar with Romantic idealism, I will provide later on in this chapter a resumé of what I understand its most salient features to be, with the intention of introducing its central ideas and illustrating how these anticipate a progressive education manifesto.

Against disinterestedness

My use of the word 'manifesto' at the end of the previous paragraph makes something else clear about this book (if this has not been obvious already): it is not remotely an impartial or disinterested one. On the contrary, while I hope its written register is suitably measured and its arguments neither prejudiced nor intolerant as a result, it has been produced to mobilize a particular bias – chiefly to reawaken interest in and encourage fresh commitment to a type of pedagogy that continues to be rhetorically influential but which struggles directly to affect teachers' practice which today is heavily circumscribed by attainment targets, performance indicators and mandated curricula. These emphases in contemporary schooling not only run counter to many teachers' naturally progressive inclinations but also connect awkwardly with those aims of education which stress children's personal growth and the development of their imaginative and creative capacities. Through restoring to teachers' critical consciousness some of the submerged, and thus mostly unacknowledged, Romantic ideas which represent how many of them *subconsciously think* about their work, the hope is that they will feel more confident both to adjust their practice in new and exciting ways and to speak the truth directly to those who currently exert so much power over it, challenging their dominant (frequently conservative) ideas with progressive alternatives. This, then, is a disruptive book that unapologetically seeks to challenge and provoke.

Utopianism and Romanticism

My effort to rehabilitate Romanticism in the service of education is paralleled in another, earlier, work of mine. Indeed, some people reading this book may realize that I have tried previously to perform a similar exercise in restoration on behalf of utopianism. In *Hope and Education* (Halpin 2003) I developed a conception of education that links being educated with the idea of *hope*, indicating the degree to which a distinctive vocabulary of optimism about schooling and teaching and learning is capable of being fostered through specific exercises of the utopian imagination. In that earlier book I argued that utopias, both generally and in education particularly, provide an important antidote to cultural pessimism, offering an alternative to currently fashionable narratives of societal and professional decline. In *Hope and Education* I also commended a particular conception of utopian realism, which defines a good utopia as one that finds a bridge between the present and the future in those forces at the current juncture which are potentially able to transform it for the better. Accordingly, educational utopians are best thought of as intellectual lookouts – that is, individuals who hypothesize an improved situation from the known historical and social facts in order to discern possibilities for future progressive action. They are not fanciful, 'wouldn't it be nice' futurists, but rather people who examine the potential for change on the basis of rigorous analyses of the likelihood and limitations of reform in the here and now.

My advocacy of utopianism and Romanticism in education does not denote two different kinds of argument. In this book they run parallel, representing, so to speak, opposite sides of the same coin. Indeed, for me, there is a sense in which being a Romantic entails sometimes simultaneously being a utopian, and vice versa, which is why, if pressed, I like to define a Romantic as someone who believes that it is better to travel hopefully than to arrive (see Brookner 2001, p. 1). Roger Simon implies the same when he remarks that

> hope is the acknowledgement of more openness in a situation than the situation easily reveals; openness above all to possibilities for human attachments, expressions and assertions ... As a particular crystal-lization of desire, hope is constituted in the need to imagine an alternative human world and to imagine it in a way that enables one to act in the present as if this alternative had already begun to emerge.
>
> (Simon 1992, pp. 4–5)

The relevance of this sentiment for education is not difficult to discern, which is why in this book I want to flip the utopian coin over so as to reveal its Romantic aspect in order to develop another, but related, progressive argument about what it means today to be a learning subject and a public educator.

People familiar with the different components that make up the Romantic vision will not find this intention remotely strange. For many of these possess utopian characteristics. Above all, as we will learn in more detail shortly, Romanticism represents a profound critique of some of modernity's most problematic and dehumanizing features, in particular its rationalistic reductionism and homogenizing technism, which it wishes to see replaced by certain foundational human values that have been marginalized in modern society – values to do with the importance of individuality, spirituality, spontaneity, feeling and emotion and community. Indeed, Romanticism's rebellion against the hegemony of technology in particular challenges us to create a utopia in which present reality is radically transformed, enabling us to live in ways that fuse together the material and the spiritual, and the mechanical and the organic, while at the some time speaking out against narrow conventionality and traditionalism. As such, to use Nikolas Kompridis' words, 'to "romanticize" the world [in this way] is to make room for the new, to make room for new possibilities' (Kompridis 2006, p. 4).

Such prospective striving is a defining characteristic of Romanticism, which is why so many of its contributors placed such high importance on dreaming – whether of the day or night variety – seeing such activity as both revelatory and anticipatory. Evidence for this valency is found throughout Blake's visionary poetry; it also, though differently, infuses aspects of Wordsworth's poetics of the unconscious (see Wilson 1993). Even Byron, who is not usually regarded as a poet of dreams, manages in his poem 'The Dream' (1816) to set down a catalogue of their functions which articulates well at this point:

> What are they?
> Creations of the mind?
> The mind can make Substance, and people planets of its own
> With beings brighter than have been seen, and give
> A breath to forms which can outlive all flesh.

Utopianism, likewise, reserves a special place for dreaming, though more often of the waking kind. As I say in *Hope in Education*:

> Utopian daydreaming ... is a significant way in which people reflect on future possibilities and in which, especially, they engage with the vicissitudes of their everyday lives, thus facilitating a degree of psychic equilibrium that helps them to resist over-deterministic interpretations of how they should be lived ... [As such] Utopian daydreams sustain life and give some direction and purpose to it ...
>
> (Halpin 2003, p. 37)

Like dreams of a sleeping kind, which show us, in Adam Philips' words, 'that there is somewhere else, somewhere beyond our sovereignty' (Philips 2003, p. 113), utopian dreams provide an opportunity to think about desired states and ways of achieving them.

This book's attempt to Romanticize education, however, is not so much about directly anticipating or daydreaming about a particular better future for it, but rather about helping those who read it to re-inherit and readmit a Romantic past into their professional lives as one means of enabling them to consider how to transform and improve the here-and-now of their work. This is not far-fetched optimism. For, as I have previously suggested, many teachers are Romantics without knowing it. Unawares, they think, if not act, with many ideas about childhood and teaching and learning that are a legacy of Romanticism, the valuing of the imaginative life and the role of the experience of love in the development of the personality being the most important. Nowadays, many educators take such ideals entirely for granted. But it was the Romantics who were among the first to bring them to our attention and to defend them. Hence, for teachers to study Romanticism now is to know better and, hopefully, to become happily reacquainted with their forgotten progressive selves (akin to meeting a long-lost friend), which may have been overtaken and overshadowed, or sometimes blotted out entirely, by ridigly prescribed polices and practices.

Philosophical argument

In the same way that I use parts of the Romantic canon as a *resource* to develop a series of linked theses about the nature of teaching and learning, philosophical argument, as commonly understood, is drawn on only to *assist* in its construction, which means this book is not strictly a 'philosophy of education' one, as that subdiscipline has historically defined such texts, though it is likely to be categorized as such. Certainly, it is not a book that analyses philosophically the meaning of particular educational words, a form of conceptual scrutiny about which I have at best agnostic feelings. I do not believe, for instance, that much of any significance is to be understood about education from an investigation of the way people commonly use such words as 'teaching', 'learning', 'discipline', 'punishment', and the rest. Stating clearly what such words mean in terms of how they are used of course is sometimes helpful, but this cannot be, for me, a substitute for saying what they *should mean at their best*. Mark Fisher is more my kind of philosopher of education. He writes, 'People can use words as they like ... I am not trying to legislate about language ... I am trying rather to reduce the welter of things to which people refer to a kind of order – *an order of preferability*' (1990, p. 39, my emphasis). In my book, as in Fisher's, there is philosophical argument, but mine, like his, takes the form of persuasive characterization.

Democracy, enhancement and personhood

Underpinning such characterization is a personal commitment to a set of educational values rooted in a higher-order principle about the role education must play in a society wanting to be democratic in ever-increasing ways. Any effective democracy needs schools to mirror ways of operating that contribute to what Basil Bernstein once referred to as pupils' 'individual enhancement', which he defined as 'the right to the means of critical understanding and to new possibilities' (2000, p. xx). Where that right is not met, or when it is curtailed or denied, neither pupils nor teachers, Bernstein concluded, will have much, if any, confidence and sense of purpose, in the absence of which it is difficult to see how either could act meaningfully and thus significantly. And without the ability to act in such ways, it is surely impossible for them to feel included or to participate, which of course are the hallmarks of a thriving democratic way of life.

Another way of outlining this is to say that while I, like Bernstein, conceive of children as learners with rights of inclusion and participation, I do this on the basis of a respect for them as *persons*. Above all else, the concept of being a person is derivative from the evaluation that individuals are agents or determiners of their own destinies, each possessing, in Richard Peters' words, 'a distinctive centre of consciousness, with peculiar feelings and purposes' (1966, p. 59). Thus, for a teacher to respect pupils as persons is to care for them, recognizing that their intentions, feelings and aspirations matter, and should therefore be taken into account, though never indulged uncritically. As Richard Pring points out:

Respect for persons is ... both an attitude and a principle. It is an attitude in the sense that one has, in recognising the other as a person, an active sympathy with how the other sees and feels about things and a detestation of the purely instrumental use or manipulation of someone else. It is a principle in that one prescribes to oneself that one should try to understand the other's point of view and how the other feels about matters.

(Pring 1984, p. 29)

The implications of this approach for pedagogy are not difficult to identify – at the very least, they challenge teachers to ask how far and in what ways they manifest in their relations with pupils an appreciation of their points of view and assist them to be similarly sensitive to each other.

Defining Romanticism

The foregrounding here of the importance of teachers respecting pupils as persons articulates well with those aspects of Romanticism which uphold the momentousness of the individual and of childhood in particular – Romantic doctrines that each stress the uniqueness or peculiarity of each person, whose essential self, especially in the case of children, is conceived of in terms which have divine associations.

Labelling such aspects as 'doctrines', however, is likely to cause consternation among those scholars of Romanticism (Connell 2001, for example) who warn against such reductive representation, arguing that the relative historical instability of the Romantic poetic canon makes drawing hard-and-fast conclusions about it highly problematic. Indeed, as Campbell reminds us, for some of these critics, the very attempt to define Romanticism goes against the spirit of the movement:

Romanticism can justifiably be presented as more of an impulse than a unified system of ideas and, what is more, an impulse toward chaos. Logically, therefore, not only is a closed definition of Romanticism not very Romantic, but, if one important aspect of Romanticism is the spirit of rebellion, then rebelling against Romanticism could also be Romantic.

(Campbell 1989, p. 179)

Such a judgement seems unnecessarily pedantic and far too pessimistic. For while Romanticism has undeniably proved hard to define, it has been even harder to get rid of, which is why I will ignore those scholars who have sought to deny its existence, because exist it does, or has existed. I side with Geoffrey Thurley, who argues: 'Even if we discredit false notions of it, we are surely obliged to admit that there is or was something which caused these effects, something which needs to be clarified and explained, not explained away' (Thurley 1983, p. 1). But there are problems, nonetheless, which need to be overcome before any sensible attempt to characterize Romanticism can get under way.

First of all, it has to be conceded that the label 'Romanticism' itself is a posthumous invention, inasmuch as none of the Romantic writers mentioned so far ever used that word (either individually or collectively) to describe their work (Butler 1981, p. 1; Perry 1998, p. 4). The history of British Romantic literature is thus dominated by a major and questionable assumption – namely that a small group of poets, with possibly Hazlitt in tow, is fully representative of 40 diverse years of literary creativity. There is also a self-serving aspect lurking behind this assumption, which goes like this: Romanticism is defined by the characteristic qualities of the work chiefly of the 'Big Six' poets; thus other work not possessing these qualities cannot be Romantic. You do not have to be clever at all to realize that this is an annular argument. As Richardson puts it: 'The notion of a "Romantic Period" ... encourages critics to extrapolate characteristic features from the textual record and then, in circular fashion, to concentrate upon those writers and texts which seem most fully to embody them' (1994, p. 3).

But even the evidence cited by those critics who propound such an argument is regarded as suspect by some commentators who insist that it is not possible to identify a sufficient amount in common between these writers to justify giving them one general name. Thus Wasserman (1964) has stated that the 'Big Six' poets 'vigorously disagreed on [many] central issues, and that their works differ in vastly more essential and interesting ways than they are similar' (p. 17). Predating Wasserman, Bate (1961) similarly concludes that 'few generalizations consistently apply to the outstanding exponents of Romanticism' (p. 164). Day observes much the same, concluding that

> attempts to summarize Romanticism inevitably end up over-system-atising and simplifying the phenomenon. They imply a coherence ... which closer inspection leads us to call into question. It is true that some of the elements by which Romanticism is defined ... do appear in the writings of those who are now called Romantic. But it is not true that all British Romantic writers display all of those elements all of the time.
>
> (Day 1996, p. 5)

These concerns, however, do not render futile the purposes of this book. Wasserman and Bate, for a start, each overstate the differences between the British Romantics, and come to a false conclusion about them as a result. And while Day asserts that British Romanticism is not constituted by a homogenous group of writers but rather by individuals among whom there are undeniable differences, he acknowledges that there are some crucial synergies between them. This seems about right, given the common structure of feeling to which each of the Romantics contributed and from which they each drew inspiration. Thus, while Shelley and Wordsworth, for example, were undoubtedly men of contrasting political persuasions, they shared between them, and with other contributors to the Romantic canon, a distinctive and common ideological outlook – one defined by Iain McCalman as a 'displacing ideal' in which they sought, in their different ways, to cope with and critique 'commercial and professional changes in the arts and letters, as well as with the ferment of national war and revolution' (2001, p. 2), not to mention the grossness of the then emergent urban society and its many dehumanizing features.

So, while I am happy to embrace Lovejoy's earlier injunction that 'we should learn to use the word "Romanticism" in the plural' (1924, p. 235), I want to hold on to the idea that there are significant intellectual and aesthetic affinities among and interrelations between my Romantics of choice, recognizing these to be neither essential nor prescriptive. Indeed, despite their embattled status, I want to argue (following McGann 1983) that, used cautiously, the terms 'Romantic' and 'Romanticism' helpfully point up certain salient features of the aesthetic ideologies of those writers, of which the 'Big Six' poets are the chief exemplars, whom today we call the 'British Romantics'.

Romanticism and Enlightenment

However, one generalization about British Romanticism that I will not be making is that which sees it as a school of thought conflicting fundamentally with Enlightenment ideas and attitudes, notably the views (associated chiefly with the philosophical outlook of the British empiricist John Locke) that knowledge is limited only to those things that can be known to the senses and which relatedly can only be reasoned about. There are two reasons for rejecting this generalization. First, it mistakenly assumes that Enlightenment rationalism was always consistent, when it was not; second, it is based on a set of false antitheses said to prevail between Romantic and Enlightenment sensibility – emotion versus reason;

individualism versus society; subjectivity versus objectivity; material versus spiritual; mechanical versus organic; rebellion versus order.

The truth of the matter is far more complex and much more interesting – a case in fact more of 'and also', rather than 'either/or', carrying the implication that Romanticism inherits many of the priorities of Enlightenment thinking, whilst augmenting them with themes it underplays or ignores. As Day points out:

> many of the preoccupations that are frequently associated with Romanticism – a perception of the stultifying effect of an unthinking imitation of tradition, the emphasis on ... the psychological capacities of the individual ... and the emphasis on feeling ... and primitive simplicity and naturalness – were [also] fundamentally Enlightenment [ones as well] ...
>
> (Day 1996, p. 76)

To that extent, like Day, I want to reject altogether the claim that the contributors to British Romanticism were saying and writing things using ideas that constituted a clean break from the dominant intellectual trends of their time. Rather, I follow Kitson, who concludes that

> [t]he canonical Romantic poets were both building upon and reacting against the thoughts of their predecessors, sometimes breaking with major trends (as in the case of Coleridge's rejection of Enlightenment empiricism) or alternatively pushing that body of thought into more extreme positions than were usual ... (as with Shelley's and Byron's radical scepticism concerning established institutions).
>
> (Kitson 1998, p. 35)

Heath and Boreham concur, arguing that

> the boundaries between the Enlightenment and Romanticism [should be understood] as blurred. Both were reforming movements, characterized by intense seriousness of purpose. The liberation of the inner man was as much the aim of the Romantics as the Enlightenment thinkers, and they both shared a sense of the absolute concepts of truth and justice being within mankind's reach ... *Romanticism* [thus conceived] *was the continuation of the Enlightenment by other means.*
>
> (Heath and Boreham 1999, p. 11, my emphasis)

Romanticism and progressive education

Other generalizations about Romanticism, most of which connect with its
status as a 'displacing ideal' (a notion defined earlier on page 20), are
easier to make, and so less problematic, though it needs to be made clear
that listing them, as I now do in the form of discrete statements below,
gives the false impression that the Romantic vision is easily pinned down
and divided up. Moreover, not all of the Romantic writers highlighted in
this book held all the views expressed in each statement with the same
degree of seriousness. And hardly any of them expressed their Romantic
views in terms which make links with teaching and learning in schools.

While not lending itself easily to systematization, and while not
adequately labelled a philosophy, I want to say that Romanticism reflects,
in its most organized form, the following five aspects:

- *A rejection of all kinds of strict rationalistic reductionism*, being hostile to any
  suggestion that a single ideological or moral outlook or dogma or
  method can be successfully applied to the solution of anything but simple
  problems. This attitude explains Hazlitt's attack on social utilitarianism,
  embracing also his vituperative assault on Thomas Malthus's theories of
  population control which he also condemned for their hypocritical
  provocations against the morality of ordinary working men and women
  (see Grayling 2000, pp. 112–16). It would also explain, if he was around
  to make it, his rejection of uniformity in curriculum provision, including
  attempts to audit the outcomes of teaching and learning using
  performance measures. He would equally be ill-tempered at the prospect
  of having to work as a teacher in a school, or any other educational
  context, in which he was systematically line-managed.
- *A rebellion against attempts to underplay the role of feeling in understanding and
  interpreting human experience*. The experience of love, Coleridge in
  particular teaches us, is crucial in this mix. Through love we fulfil
  our individuality, deriving through loving experience the renewal of
  self, brought about by the special bond it fosters between ourselves and
  other people, whom we value equally as ourselves and with whom we
  seek to become united. Because love, at its best, is neither selfish nor
  controlling, and because it does not necessarily entail affectionate
  physical relationships, its relevance to teaching well should not be
  ignored. Certainly, it brings into sharp relief the ways in which a
  progressive pedagogy in which sympathy for the child's point of view is
  given high priority might be worked out in practice.
- *A negative attitude towards all attempts to drive a wedge between reason and*

imagination, the sensitive harmonizing of which for the Romantics represents a form of perfection. Indeed, being an artist for many of the Romantics (Shelley in particular) was about embodying this attitude – especially about using one's creative imagination to overcome insensibility, notably of a moral kind. In the same way that the Romantics sought personal renewal through the power of writing poetry, so the progressive teacher encourages intellectual rejuvenation through involving pupils in learning tasks that stretch and develop their creative and imaginative abilities, and which, as a result, as with the Romantics, fosters a high degree of emotional engagement with the material and natural world. Indeed, such engagement, which rejects telling and instruction in favour of sensitizing and strengthening feelings, realizes in pupils an ideal responsiveness to pleasure, causing them joy.

- *An oppositional attitude about all forms of traditionalism for its own sake*, especially where this takes the form of legitimating the privileges of the powerful and the hegemony of philistine forms of professionalism and vocationalism. In much the same way that the Romantics represent the main conceptual alternative to the emerging technological and economic world-view of their time, so progressive educators today remind us of the importance of investing in education in ways that do not see it exclusively as a narrow preparation for the world of work, but as one of the many ways in which young people can be helped to explore a wide variety of possibilities in life.

- *An insubordinate, heroic sometimes, commitment to challenging the ugliness, spiritual emptiness and crude materialism of modern life*, reflected in the progressive educator's need to flout and confront approaches to teaching and learning which are overly prescriptive and narrowly conceived in terms of the aims of education they seek to promote, requiring them to be courageous and tenacious in defying conventions that are entangled with powerful vested interests.

The Romantic character: energy and power

The philosopher Isaiah Berlin described Romanticism as 'the greatest single shift in the consciousness of the West that has occurred in the course of the nineteenth and twentieth centuries' (1999, p. 1). This seems an exaggerated evaluation, since aspects of Romanticism have featured throughout cultural history, and so did not therefore require a relatively recent, short and discrete period of years of English literary activity to bring it into existence.

On the other hand, Berlin is surely right to argue that British literary poetic Romanticism, alongside continental Romantic movements in drama, music, painting, philosophy, sculpture and architecture, ushered in a quite extraordinary structure of feeling during the 50 years or so after 1785 (Porter and Teich 1988). This opposed, chiefly on general human grounds, the kind of civilization that was at the time being brought into existence by increased industrialization and concomitant urbanization, which together made awful the condition of many people's lives. All of this, in Raymond Williams' words, 'passed into our common experience, to lie there, formulated and unformulated, to move and to be examined' (1961, p. 64).

What has passed less into our corporate historical memory is the detail of the personalities who were involved in creating this common experience, whose biographies and characters sometimes say as much about the nature of British Romanticism as the specific artistic and other creative work they produced, which is why in the rest of this chapter I want to touch on the extraordinary force of will and energy that two of its main contributors – Hazlitt and Coleridge – brought to their art.

Hazlitt and Coleridge were serious and intense, sometimes melancholy, people, who pursued their beliefs to the limit, and in ways that eventually brought them into violent conflict with one another and with other people. In my final chapter, drawing mostly on Hazlitt's writings, I will indicate how this kind of earnestness represents an exemplary and exciting way of being a public intellectual. For now, I want to focus more on the personalities and outlooks of these writers, and how they anticipate ways in which both teachers and learners might operate more effectively.

A good way of becoming acquainted with Hazlitt is to examine his image as represented in a head-and-shoulders self-portrait which he produced in his 25th year, in 1813. This painting is reproduced on the cover of several books written about him, including two recent ones – Anthony Grayling's (2000) biography, *The Quarrel of the Age*, and Tom Paulin's (1998) *The Day-Star of Liberty*, which is a study of Hazlitt's literary style. As Grayling says, this painting is 'a striking piece of biographical evidence' (p. 76), in which we can glimpse many of Hazlitt's personal characteristics, manifest at the time when the portrait was produced, which remained with him throughout his relatively short life: his single-mindedness (as reflected in the direct way he stares out of the portrait); and his vulnerability, intelligence, pride and loneliness (as shown in his unsmiling mouth and brooding eyes). It is, concludes Grayling, 'the face of a young man prone to shyness and romantic dreams, but at the same time strongly confident in his judgements' – someone possessing a 'strong sense of [his] superior mental power [which] is discernible in the haunting broad-browed face with its luminously searching eyes' (2000, p. 76). Paulin is struck by those eyes as well: 'there is something raw, unformed, even dangerous, in his direct, but somehow vulnerably shrouded gaze' (1998, p. 1).

Further contemporary insight into Hazlitt's character, this time as a middle-aged intellectual, is provided by John Clare, arguably England's greatest labouring-class poet. He first met Hazlitt – of whom he was already a great admirer, but only by reputation – in July 1823. Clare was just 30; Hazlitt, 45. The occasion was a publishers' dinner held in Fleet Street, at which Coleridge, as guest of honour, and the brilliant essayist Thomas de Quincey were also present. Although the dominant personality of the evening was Coleridge (who used it as an opportunity to deliver one of his customary overly-long monologues), it was Hazlitt who caught Clare's attention the most, and who caused him to write this short pen-portrait:

> He sits in a silent picture of severity – if you was [*sic*] to watch his face for a month you would not catch a smile there – his eyes were always turned towards the ground except when one is turned up and then with a sneer that cuts a bad pun and a young author's maiden table-talk to atoms wherever it is directed ... when he enters a room he comes stooping with his eyes in his hands as if it were throwing under gazes round at every corner as if he smelt a dun [a creditor] or thief ready to seize him by the collar and demand his money or his life. He is a middle-sized dark-looking man and his face is deeply-lined with a satirical character ... For the blood of me I could not find him out, that is I should have had no guess at him of his ever being a scribbler, much more a genius'.
>
> (Bate 2003, pp. 264–5)

But literary genius he was, despite many of the somewhat unappealing features to which Clare here draws attention, some more than likely being the product of the extremely hostile state into which Hazlitt's friendship with Coleridge had fallen by this time, and maybe too because he was simply bored by the latter's overbearing lecturing style.

While 20 years apart, the image projected by Hazlitt's self-portrait and the later remembrances of a contemporaneous artist each draw attention to his intense, brooding intelligence, and its magnetic, seductive almost, effect, which operated alongside his many flaws, notably his aloofness and arrogance. Moreover, despite his formidable intelligence, Hazlitt could be deeply stupid (for instance, in his incorrigible infatuations with younger women), and at times his judgement was poor (for example, his absurdly uncritical assessment of Napoleon). He was in fact an extraordinary mix of a man – awkward, shy and unstable, yet also passionate, brilliant and authoritative.

Hazlitt had many admirers and friends, one of whom, Peter Patmore, also a confidant, though never an uncritical one, described his mental alertness in these terms: 'Hazlitt could perceive and describe "at sight" the characteristics of anything without any previous study or knowledge whatever, but by a species of intellectual intuition' (Epstein 1991, p. 2). Hazlitt's absolute integrity, led him to hate hypocrites and time-servers in equal measure, and to always stand by his own principles, to the point sometimes of being obdurate in defending them, and in ways that made some people despair of him, though not in a fashion that made him entirely uncritical of himself. We will learn more about this aspect of Hazlitt's character in Chapter 7.

Leigh Hunt, one of Hazlitt's publishers, elicited in this context a famous and typical reaction. Exasperated on one occasion by Hazlitt's intellectual obstinacy, Hunt presented him with a piece of paper on which he had listed some of his faults. The story has it that Hazlitt read the list through very carefully, after which he exclaimed, 'By God, sir, there's a good deal of truth in it' (Whelan 2003, p. 186). And there probably was. Indeed, Hazlitt expected of himself as much as he expected of other people, which was a great deal, centring more often than not on the requirement that they should live their lives earnestly and honestly, making the best possible use of their talents and never offering feeble excuses for failing to live up to them. In a world made up of 'life-enhancers', on the one hand, and 'life-detractors', on the other, it was of the former group, and never the latter, that Hazlitt was a fully paid-up permanent member.

Hazlitt's enthusiasm for life led him, despite all the personal, professional and financial troubles which he endured, to count his life as having been a happy one. This enthusiasm, reflected in his curiosity and openness to experience and new ideas, made him often marvellous company, and always an effective raconteur. Almost inventing the word 'gusto', he certainly embodied it more than many intellectuals of the time, and indeed maybe since. Whelan writes that his abiding sense of Hazlitt

is of a man aware of a rich and complex inner life; a man capable of love and hate; a man who was both very fragile and extraordinarily robust;

a human being with an irrepressible masculinity together with an unmanly, feminine gentleness of mind; a strident adult taking on the world around him; an infant on the edge of a precipice in desperate need of love and support.

(Whelan 2003, p. 186)

I agree, too, albeit in a qualified way, with the inscription on Hazlitt's recently restored gravestone in St Anne's churchyard, Soho, which sums him up thus: 'A despiser of the merely Rich and Great. A Lover of the People, poor or Oppressed. A Man of true moral courage ... He lived and died the unconquered Champion of Truth, Liberty and Humanity'. Ronald Blythe, the literary critic, goes further, describing Hazlitt as 'the spokesman for the inarticulate, the exploited, the self-deceived and less brave inhabitants of George IV's England – the conscience of an era' (Blythe 1970, p. 35). However, this is not quite accurate, as Hazlitt was rarely, if ever, a direct champion of the poor and downtrodden, whom he often disparaged, being more (in the words of the Marxist historian E.P. Thompson) a 'middle-class radical [who] aimed his polemic, not towards the popular, but towards the polite culture of his time' (1968, pp. 820–1). While this is true in a way, it does not detract ultimately from his overall contribution, which was significant, as endorsed by Michael Foot, one-time Leader of the British Labour Party and persistent Hazlitt advocate, about whom he has said: 'A whole curriculum of schooling for reformers could be compiled from the writings of Hazlitt whom the nervous nineteenth century would have preferred to have dismissed as a wayward romantic essayist' (1986, p. 94). For sure, Hazlitt was sometimes 'wayward'; but for certain as well he was always, and thankfully and instructively, sincerely 'Romantic'.

Much the same can be said of Coleridge, Wordsworth referring to him once as 'the most wonderful man' he had ever known (see Sisman 2000). Not everyone who came into contact with Coleridge, however, was equally impressed: critics in his lifetime and since drawing attention to his opium addiction, his plagiarism, his marital infidelity, his political faithlessness and his naïve religiosity. Undoubtedly, these weaknesses were writ large in Coleridge's life, thus making him a difficult personality for many people today to admire, least of all to like and to consider learning much from. In fact one of Coleridge's fiercest critics in his own lifetime (as I make clear in Chapter 7) was Hazlitt who, after having once been a close friend and confidant, condemned him politically as an apostate and intellectually as a loose and empty thinker.

However, despite all this, appreciated in his entirety, and despite

Hazlitt's final and accurate unflattering evaluation, Coleridge ends up – for this appreciator, anyhow – a controversial personality, yes, but also an admirable genius – someone who possessed an electrifying creativity and a surplus of boundless intellectual energy. And we can thank a recently published biography of him – Richard Holmes' fabulously written two-volume study (1999a and 1999b) – for helping to recreate him in this more complimentary light for a modern readership. Holmes reminds us that, in addition to helping to bring about a revolution in literary taste and sensibility, Coleridge was also

> a journalist of genius, a translator, a matchless letter-writer ... an incomparable autobiographer and self-interrogator in his *Notebooks* ... a literary critic, a spectacular lecturer, a folklorist, a philosopher, a psychologist ... a playwright and a dramatic critic, and ... a metaphysician. He was also a travel-writer, a fell-walker, and amateur naturalist with an inspired eye for movement and transformation processes – cloud structures, plant growth, animal activity, light shifts, water changes, wind effects.
>
> (Holmes 1999a, p. xv)

If, like me, you find it exhausting merely to think about Holmes' affirmative profile of Coleridge's overall impact, what, I wonder, would it have been like actually to meet and know the man? Draining, tiring and testing, more than likely, as was certainly the case also with Hazlitt. For, like Hazlitt, Coleridge was a 'larger than life' personality, who frustrated and irritated many of his contemporaries, reminding one of the famous Tibetan saying which goes a bit like this: 'It is better to have lived one day as a tiger than a thousand years as a sheep.' To 'know' Coleridge and Hazlitt, even at the distance of almost two centuries, I think is to appreciate the truth of this aphorism, and in this context it has implications, not just for living one's life well, but also for being an effective teacher and learner.

Let me briefly highlight what I mean by the last part of this larger claim, by recalling some of the single words I have used in this chapter to describe the Romantic personalities of Hazlitt and Coleridge. They included:

intelligent
brave
boundless
passionate
authoritative

earnest
honest
enthusiastic
open
energetic
creative
controversial.

While acknowledging the masculine roots of some of these words, each, progressively defined, makes a fine epithet for both 'teaching' and 'learning', as aspects of all of the chapters which follow I hope will indicate, highlighting in particular how they illuminate what is meant by an 'effective' teacher and an 'effective' learner. Indeed, the collision of both attitudes, articulating with specific renderings of each or most of the words identified above, arguably, is a necessary condition for bringing into existence an educational experience warranting the label 'authentic'. Of course, no single teacher can expect, professionally, to enact fully, day-by-day, or over a career even, what these words point up. Rather, it is enough that teachers should merely bear these words in mind, working out how best they might apply them to what they do in promoting pupil learning and redefining themselves professionally. Likewise, pupils themselves, through the encouragement of their teachers, may be helped to embody them in the course of their lives and learning.

The appeal to teachers increasingly to lead their professional lives in such a way brings to my mind the dire experience of achieving the opposite – specifically, the experience of teaching a bad lesson, and knowing it. For me, such moments, apart from being acutely embarrassing, have always represented a kind of dying (analogous, I suppose, to the experience stage actors have when they fluff their lines or when musicians play a wrong note or come in too late or too early). Reflecting on such moments, as I write now, I am reminded of the ways both Hazlitt and Coleridge are said to have literally died – with the former declaiming, seemingly against every empirical fact, that he had lived a 'happy' life, and by the former, as he slipped into painful oblivion, that he 'could even be witty'. Maybe neither man said either of these things. Even if they did not, one can easily imagine they might have, for they fit the kinds of people they were: always optimistic and largely without regret, sets of words that may need to be added to the long list I offered above, pointing up the degree to which teaching and learning well sometimes require a special kind of nerve and resolve, complemented by earnestness. Certainly, they inform the approach I have adopted in developing the arguments set down in this book, the content of the rest of which is written in six chapters, and as follows.

Chapter 2 reflects on Romantic images of childhood, each of which, it is argued, has profound implications for how teachers should define and regard pupils as effective learners; then, Chapter 3, which is the most historical one in the book, examines the school experiences of two particular Romantic writers – Hazlitt and Wordsworth – drawing out what these teach us about contemporary teaching and learning in schools. Meanwhile, Chapter 4 addresses a big idea in Romanticism – that of Love – which is used as the basis for developing an argument about the need for and form and content of a mode of loving pedagogy. Subsequently, the pedagogical significance of Romantic heroism and imagination are explored separately in Chapters 5 and 6 respectively. The final chapter – Chapter 7 – which precedes a short summary conclusion, provides insight into how Romantic criticism might inform the role that education public intellectuals should play at the current juncture, both within the academy and the wider society.

2

Romantic Images of Childhood: From Innocence to Transcendence

The Child is father of the man,
And I could wish my days to be
Bound each to each by natural piety.

(William Wordsworth)

The emergence of childhood

The Romantic period in this country did not give rise to any one dominant view of childhood, but rather a variety of them. Even so, it was incontrovertibly a time when concepts of childhood, and their implications for education, were much argued about. In all probability it is also the period from which we can date the origins of many of today's taken-for-granted attitudes about children's natures. Certainly that is the impression of Cunningham (1995), whose study of representations of childhood in Western societies since the sixteenth century concludes that it is from about 1750 that we can date in England the beginnings of what is assumed to be a singular 'truth' about being a child – that it is a chapter in people's lives that, willy-nilly, *continuously informs* how they think, feel and act in their adult years.

Some of the Romantic writers whose work features in this book played no small part in aiding this process, thus giving credence to the view expressed by Richardson in his important cultural history of education in late-eighteenth- and early-nineteenth-century England that 'it is to a large extent through [their work] that childhood gained the central position it continues to hold in the Western cultural tradition' (1994, p. 9). Cunningham agrees, highlighting the degree to which this new status sets out an ideal of childhood in which 'it was transformed from being [merely] a preparatory phase in the making of an adult to being the *spring* which should nourish the whole of life' (1995, p. 73, my emphasis). Because the Romantics often regarded adulthood as a time in which people had sadly mislaid the spark of their youth, this ideal was often expressed nostalgically, using utopian categories. Here is Cunningham again:

> From the time of the Romantic poets onwards it is not uncommon to see childhood as a repository of inheritances and attributes which were often lost or blunted in adulthood. The more adults and adult society seemed bleak, urbanized and alienated, the more childhood came to be seen as properly a garden, enclosing within the safety of its walls a way of life which was in touch with nature and which preserved the rude virtues of earlier periods of the history of mankind.
>
> (Cunningham 1991, p. 43)

The hold on our thinking that any conception of childhood has is crucial. For how children are contemplated is highly consequential for how we think they should, for example, be best reared in the family and properly tutored in school. In another important sense, the manner in which childhood is constituted mirrors ideas we have about the society we live in, including its prospects. As Chris Jenks observes in his sociological study of the phenomenon,

> from the earliest Socratic dialogue, onwards through the history of ideas, moral, social and political theorists have systematically endeavoured to constitute a view of the child that is compatible with their particular visions of social life and continuous with their speculations concerning the future.
>
> (Jenks 1996, p. 2)

Indeed, this compatibility can even seem on occasions to be a synergy, particularly when politicians, as is now often and increasingly the case, conceive of the parenting and education of children in ways that relate them to the destiny and well-being of society, justifying all manner of initiatives, to enhance and protect their status and rights. Nicholas Rose, in his study of the growth of control over personhood during the previous century, argues that 'the modern child has become the focus of innumerable projects that purport to safeguard it from physical, sexual and moral danger, to ensure its "normal" development, to actively promote certain capacities of attributes such as intelligence, educability and emotional stability' (Rose 1989, p. 43).

This chapter will explore the contribution made by some of the British Romantics to the business of defining what a child is and what childhood is about, looking specifically at Wordsworth's 'transcendental' view of infancy, which is discussed via an appreciation of Blake's earlier estimation of its essential 'innocence', assessing their relevance jointly for contemporary educational times. The chapter continues, however, with some important further scene-setting, including the recalling of an associated Swiss influence. The former is provided by another historian of the times, Lawrence Stone, who helpfully identifies the different views about childhood prevalent in the period 1740–1800; the latter, by the eighteenth-century social philosopher and writer Jean-Jacques Rousseau, whose book *Emile* (first issued in 1762) includes a highly influential attempt to develop a psychology of childhood, accompanied by a treatise on how children should ideally be brought up in the home and educated. Finally, I will reflect upon how the Romantics' ideas on childhood might illuminate current education debates.

Four views of childhood

Histories of any idea are unlikely to satisfy all people equally, particularly if they embody attempts to 'periodize', even mildly, the ascendancy of one view and the rise and fall of another. For this reason alone, we need to be aware that historical divisions are in reality fairly fluid. Ideas, including the structures of feeling with which they are associated, never emerge spontaneously out of the air; nor are they completely abandoned as others begin to overtake them. Continuities and overlappings, rather than discontinuities and sharp breaks, are more frequently the manner of things.

That being the case, it seems clear that at least four views about childhood were prevalent in England in the 150 years leading up to the beginning of the nineteenth century. Lawrence Stone's (1979) extensive study, *The Family, Sex and Marriage in England 1500–1800*, provides an account of each of them.

His first view, and the one that commended itself to most people at the time, was the *traditional Christian* attitude, strongly buttressed by Calvinist theology, that the child is born with original sin, and that the only prospect therefore of saving it from moral self-destruction through its self-gratifying pursuit of dangerous pleasures is by the most ruthless repression of its will, requiring the subject to be strictly controlled by his parents, teachers and all others in authority over him. This religious view, it needs to be said quickly, legitimated the then commonplace sentiment that with or without God's involvement, all inferiors, of which children were seen as prime examples, must always, and without question, subject themselves to the authority of their superiors. Accordingly, obedience and deference were the order of the day in an eighteenth-century English society considered by its members to be naturally and inevitably hierarchical.

Parenting consequently consisted of distant and strict moral guidance, more often than not enforced by a regime of unremitting discipline, including corporal punishment. James *et al.* express this attitude in terms reminiscent of Michel Foucault's *Discipline and Punish*: 'Childhood, the context within which the otherness of the child [was] rendered safe, [was] ... shaped by the exercise of restraint on [its base] dispositions ... [giving] rise to docile adult bodies ... good citizens, pliant members of the social order' (1998, p. 10).

Charles Dickens is a great source for tales of institutionalized brutality in childrearing. Mr Murdstone's harsh treatment of the child David Copperfield, for example, is justified by him under such a regime: 'the gloomy theology of the Murdstones made all children out to be a swarm of vipers'; while Arthur Clenham, in *Little Dorrit*, is a man whose will is systematically broken during the wretched childhood he lives out under his mother's fanatical Calvinism. Meanwhile, the child Pip in *Great Expectations* is the subject of philosophical speculations at the Gargery dinner-table: 'Why is it that the young are never grateful?', someone asks rhetorically, only for the reply to be forthcoming that they are 'naturally vicious', to which all present assent with a murmured 'True!'. The Romantics, had they been present, would have disagreed strongly, which is why you will not find the Christian attitude to childhood featuring at all in any of their writings, other than negatively. On the other hand, the politics of restraint on the very young with which it was associated in Dickens' time has contemporary resonances, echoing, for example, in past policies for 'short sharp shocks', aimed at bringing to heel recalcitrant youth, and in more recent appeals to allow teachers and parents to smack children if they think this is necessary to curb their misbehaviour.

Stone's second view is the *environmentalist* one: 'that a child is born with a natural disposition towards neither good nor evil, but is [rather] a *tabula rasa* [blank page], malleable and consequently open to being moulded by experience' (Stone 1979, p. 406). This view was given wide currency by the influential empiricist philosopher John Locke, whose *An Essay Concerning Human Understanding*, published in 1690, advanced the then revolutionary thesis that all the concepts possessed by humankind are given in experience. Accordingly, there was, on this basis, nothing predetermined about childhood, a period of time during which children's minds, characters and personalities could be influenced for the better, depending upon the nature of the experiences to which they were exposed, or in Coleridge's schema 'associated'. In his subsequent bestseller, *Some Thoughts upon Education* (it went into an astonishing 26 British editions alone before 1800), Locke translated his empiricism into a set of child-centred maxims about the educational process, giving it a positive social-engineering role, in the course of which children are socialized into 'gentlemanly' modes of behaviour.

The publication of Locke's tract on education coincided, significantly, with a period in English history during which a lessening of deferential and hierarchical attitudes became apparent (evidenced, for example, in the events of the 1688 'English Revolution', which led to the rejection of the principle of Divine Right of Kings and the doctrine of passive obedience, and to the passage of a Bill of Rights). To that extent, its proposals were fit for the times. This, however, did not prevent the Romantics from being sceptical, to the point of hostility, about the sort of rationalist approaches to education to which Locke's approach gave legitimacy. They criticized them for being overly concerned with instruction and the mere passing on of factual knowledge and inert ideas at the expense of fostering a critical form of aesthetic intelligence. Such criticism did little to prevent the environmentalist view becoming, by the beginning of the nineteenth century, the most supported one, supplanting by a long way, but not entirely replacing, the orthodox Christian attitude. It still of course exerts residual influence on some of today's teachers, who continue to define class 'work' as a matter largely of filling up pupils' empty minds with important information, which they must copy down, memorize and periodically recall.

Stone's third view is the *biological* one: 'that the character and potentialities of the child are genetically determined at conception' (Stone 1979, p. 406), and that therefore there is very little either a parent or a teacher can do to alter things, other than to reinforce good habits and eliminate bad ones. Although this view is not directly related to the earlier Christian one, there are some obvious resemblances, inasmuch as both are characterized by a fatalistic prospectus, though in this biological case the responses to it are not so harsh. For being educated under its guise was seen as a matter of developing and consolidating what the child already has, which if it is very little is just too bad. This view of childhood, not surprisingly, does not feature positively at all in the work of the 'Big Six' poets, or in the essays of Hazlitt. However, like the previous environmentalist attitude, it does crop up from time to time in contemporary teacher discourse in the form of statements that some children are, by definition, impossible to educate well, given their poor backgrounds, family histories, and inadequate starts in life.

Stone's fourth and last view is the *utopian* one: 'that the child is born good and is corrupted only by his experience in society' (Stone 1979, p. 406). In this schema, the young child is angelic, innocent and untainted by the world which it has recently entered. It has, in Jenks' words,

> a natural goodness and a clarity of vision that we might 'idolize' or even 'worship' as the source of all that is best in human nature ... Such children play and chuckle, smile and laugh, both spontaneously but also with our sustained encouragement ... [Thus] children in this image are not curbed [as in the 'biological' view] nor beaten into submission [as in the 'Christian' one], they are ... enabled and facilitated.
>
> (Jenks 1996, p. 73).

My use of the word 'worship' a moment ago, moreover, provides the Romantic connection, specifically a link with Wordsworth, and before him Blake, each of whom, as we shall learn, informed childhood with a divine or quasi-divine nature, giving it a status superior to adulthood.

Rousseau's *Emile*

The first formalization of the utopian child, however, predates both Blake and Wordsworth, occurring with Rousseau. His landmark manifesto *Emile* (1762; see Jimack 1974) sought to reveal the child's innate nature and immanent capacity for reason, which in each case he invested with 'organic' principles of growth that can be either distorted or fostered by primary socialization and by formal education. Rousseau's attempt to capture something of the 'naturalness' of childhood was quite simply revolutionary at the time of its publication, notwithstanding the fact that his was an age in which more intellectuals than hitherto were offering up increasingly sensitive responses to the natural world in general (see Porter 1982, pp. 284–8).

In breaking new ground in people's thinking about childhood, child-rearing and the education of children, *Emile* was innovatory in three ways. First, it advocated that the child should learn chiefly from experience and nature rather than from books and instruction: 'Childhood has its own ways of seeing, thinking and feeling'; it is 'the sleep of reason' (Rousseau, in Jimack 1974, p. 44). Educators, Rousseau insists, should therefore give up on Locke's rationalist approach to teaching and learning. For while his image of childhood stresses the importance of learning from experience, it privileges (wrongly) the teacher's view of things, rather than the child's.

Instead of seeking to imprint on the mind of the child particular habits of thinking and acting compatible with becoming an adult, children, Rousseau argues, should, instead, be allowed to *discover for themselves, and in their own terms*, the secret of true happiness, albeit guided (we'd say 'enabled' or 'assisted' today) by a kindly tutor.

Second, *Emile* reinforced newly emerging attitudes to child-rearing, giving further publicity to new sensibilities surrounding motherhood, stressing the importance of maternal breast-feeding and swaddling. And, third, it asserted, most importantly of all, *the right of a child to be a child*, and for it to be allowed to be content in this status, arguing that childhood is the best time of a person's life, something to be looked back upon with happy memory:

> Love childhood, indulge its sports, its delightful instincts. Who has not sometimes regretted [the passing of] that age when laughter was ever on the lips, and when the heart was ever at peace? Why rob these innocents of the joys which pass so quickly, of that precious gift which they cannot abuse? Why fill with bitterness the fleeting days of early childhood, days which will no more return for them than for you?
>
> (Rousseau, in Jimack 1974, p. 43)

This attitude is far removed from the earlier Christian image of childhood which derided the infant as a sinfully disposed nonbeing, anticipating today's dominant view that accords children both rights and social standing. As James *et al.* argue: 'Through *Emile*, the child was promoted to the status of a person, a specific class of being with needs and desires and even rights. And it is this personification which has paved the way for our contemporary concern about children as individuals' (1998, p. 13).

William Blake: innocence and experience

The concept of childhood's original innocence (and the idea of it being central to the search for selfhood) was taken up and developed further by several of the Romantic poets, most notably Blake and Wordsworth. In their comparable, though radically distinctive ways, each argued for a view of the child, and also of society, that went beyond the narrow rationalism and instrumentalism favoured by the followers of Locke. In addition, their images of childhood and education represented an indirect critique of the industrialization and associated urbanization which they observed at the time, the dehumanizing effects of which they found appalling, and from which they believed people could be partly rescued by keeping alive the repressed child within each of them.

Blake's *Songs of Innocence*, published in 1789, is the first and fullest expression of this characteristically Romantic position on childhood innocence, including adulthood's decline from the freshness of spirit and outlook characteristic of the infant years. Indeed, the book's subtitle, *Showing the Two Contrary States of the Human Soul*, signals clearly its author's intention, which is to liberate the limitations of adult consciousness through a recovery of the key characteristics of childhood innocence. Its introductory frontispiece does the same in a pictorial way, depicting a shepherd with his pipe, pausing from singing, clearly led and inspired by the winged infant flying overhead in a pink cloud, who is seen instructing him to write down his songs so that all may read them.

The appeal to children of such imagery at this point and elsewhere in the book is not accidental. For Blake, at the time, was working in the tradition of writing verse for *both* adult and child readership. Indeed, the Romantic era saw a huge increase in the number of texts published for children, including chapbook tales of magic, courage, cunning, strength and endurance (see Richardson 1994 and McGavran 1991). To that extent, Blake's attempt to appeal in *Songs of Innocence* to both kinds of reader simultaneously may be regarded as an effort by him to represent in prose and art what he thinks should be the case – namely, a unity of spirit between the child and the adult in each of us, albeit with the former rather than the latter in the lead, which, for him, is pathologically the reverse of things ordinarily.

Blake develops his main theme immediately in the Introduction to the *Songs of Innocence*, where he characterizes himself, the creative poet, as a piper, then a singer, and finally a writer – each in turn inspired by the swiftly passing, ephemeral wishes of a laughing child as muse:

> Piping down the valleys wild,
> Piping songs of pleasant glee,
> On a clod I saw a child,
> And he laughing said to me:
>
> 'Pipe a song about a lamb!'
> So I piped with merry cheer,
> 'Piper, pipe that song again';
> So I piped; he wept to hear.
>
> 'Drop thy pipe, thy happy pipe
> Sing thy songs of happy chear':

So I sung the same again,
While he wept with joy to hear.

'Piper, sit thee down and write
'In a book that all may read.'
So he vanish'd from my sight,
And I pluck'd a hollow reed,

And I made a rural pen,
And I stain'd the water clear,
And I wrote my happy songs
Every child may joy to hear.

(Bronowski 1958, p. 26)

This simple poem acts as a sort of manifesto of the role of the Romantic poet, whose main aesthetic purpose is to refresh in readers' minds the spirit of innocence, recapturing the fleeting moment of imaginative vision. The remaining poems in the *Songs of Innocence* have this as their common theme, finding expression in a variety of written registers and moods, ranging from sadness, anger and fear ('The Little Black Boy'; 'The Chimney Sweeper'; 'The Little Boy Lost'), to carefree, joyful enthusiasm and optimism ('The Little Boy Found'; 'Laughing Song'; 'Infant Joy').

However, one poem in the collection, 'Nurse's Song', brings to the fore better than any other in the book the innocence of childhood which Blake is so concerned to applaud and to which he is most anxious to draw people's attention:

When the voices of children are heard on the green,
And Laughing is heard on the hill,
My heart is at rest within my breast
And everything else is still.

'Then come home my children, the sun is gone down
And the dews of night arise;
Come, come, leave off play, and let us away
Till the morning appears in the skies.'

'No, no, let us play, for it is yet day
And we cannot go to sleep;
Besides, in the sky the little birds fly,
And the hills are all covered with sheep.'

'Well, well, go and play till the light fades away,
And then go home to bed.'
The little ones leaped and shouted and laughed
And all the hills echoéd.

The children's nurse here, representing a form of adult consciousness, follows their wishes, allowing them to continue playing until tiredness finally sets in. She talks empathically with the children, complementing her experience with theirs.

In another poem with the same name, published in *Songs of Experience*, Blake shows us the reverse of this attitude:

When the voices of children are heard on the green,
And whisperings are in the dale,
The days of my youth rise fresh in my mind,
My face turns green and pale.

Then come home, my children, the sun is gone down,
And the dews of night arise;
Your spring and your day are wasted in play,
And your winter and night in disguise.

The mood here is entirely different: there is no sympathetic communication between the nurse and the children; instead, there are only guilty inferences ('whisperings are in the dale'); while the nurse's own sufferings in youth are used by her as an excuse to limit the children's opportunities, culminating in her cynical observation that their playfulness is, in any event, a form of time-wasting.

These antithetical poems clearly illustrate Blake's effort to transform the meaning and status of youthful innocence, through the power of his artistry, connecting him fully to the discussion that follows which centres on how childhood is constituted in quasi-theological terms in the poetry of Wordsworth.

Wordsworth's transcendental child

Fifty years after the publication of Rousseau's *Emile*, on 26 March 1802, Wordsworth wrote the following poem:

> My heart leaps up when I behold
> A rainbow in the sky:
> So was it when my life began;
> So it is now I am a man;
> So be it when I shall grow old,
> Or let me die!
> The Child is father of the man,
> And I could wish my days to be
> Bound each to each by natural piety.

No other work of Wordsworth's so perfectly embodies his conception of the life-span and the meaning of personal identity within it. Indeed, it expresses a major Wordsworthian theme – namely, that the self continues as a single identity from the past, across the present and into the future. Significantly, given the concerns of this chapter, in a reverse of the usual paternal origin, the experience of the child, Wordsworth tells us, is the foundation upon which adult identity is based.

But there is a lot more to say about this. For Wordsworth's appreciation of the sovereignty of individual identity across time, and of the primordiality of childhood in the patterning of human experience, articulates with another key idea in his oeuvre: that of infancy positively endowed with blessings from God. In his oft-quoted 'Intimations of Immortality' (1804), a poem whose influence on nineteenth-century conceptions of childhood is arguably as great as that of Freud's on present-day ones (Cunningham 1995, p. 74), Wordsworth, taking his cue most certainly from Platonic philosophy (and maybe from Rousseau too), conceives of the child as 'apparelled in celestial light':

> Our birth is but a sleep and a forgetting:
> The Soul that rises with us, our life's Star,
> Hath had elsewhere its setting,
> And cometh from afar:
> Not in entire forgetfulness,
> And not in utter nakedness,
> But trailing clouds of glory do we come
> From God, who is our home:
> Heaven lies about us in our infancy!

Children here do not possess original sin. Quite the opposite – they are equipped with keener perceptions of beauty and truth than adults. The child is not an empty vessel waiting to be filled up with adult knowledge, but rather,

> Mighty prophet! Seer blest
> On whom those truths do rest
> Which we are toiling all our lives to find.

In short, the child is God's agent and conduit, possessing divine status and almost warranting worship.

Wordsworth elaborates further on this major theme in *The Prelude*, where at one point he revisits his thinking about the essential link between childhood imaginative experience and adult creativity:

> There are in our existence spots of time
> That with distinct pre-eminence retain
> A fructifying virtue, whence, depressed
> By trivial occupations and the round
> Of ordinary intercourse, our minds –
> Especially the imaginative power –
> Are nourished and invisibly repaired.
> (*The Prelude* Book 1, 288–94)

What Wordsworth is describing here is an associative process in the mind, whereby, in adulthood, images within it are revisited and revised, contributing to new imaginative feelings such as the child could not have had.

The progress of our existential imaginative selves, however, has its starting point in infancy – at the mother's breast:

> ... blest the babe
> Nursed in his mother's arms, the babe who sleeps
> Upon his mother's breast, who when his soul
> Claims manifest kindred with an earthly soul
> Does gather passion from his mother's eye.

Such feelings

> ... pass into his torpid life
> Like an awakening breeze, and hence his mind,
> Even in the first trial of its powers,
> Is prompt and watchful...
> (Book 2, 269–77)

The child, then, from his earliest days, is full of imaginative being, capable at once of creation and perception. An 'agent of the one great mind' (God), he performs the highest imaginative act – that is, 'a repetition in the finite mind of the eternal act of creation in the Infinite I AM'.

For Wordsworth, life's passage is not a gradual ascent from naïve childhood to adult maturity, but rather the reverse – a decline from the vividness and immediacy of infancy – 'Our birth is but a sleep and a forgetting' – which he regards as the best part of life, declaring memorably that 'heaven lies about us in our infancy'.

But these aspects of childhood need not be lost as we age. On the contrary, the spark of infancy can be re-ignited, providing we remain open to its powers. So, earlier in the 'Immortality Ode', we read of Wordsworth's melancholy about his fading creative abilities in early middle age, a mood from which he quickly rescues himself by recalling the 'brightness' of youth, which he allows to illuminate and regenerate his imaginative thinking in the here and now:

It is not now as it has been of yore;
Turn wheresoe'er I may,
By night or day,
The Things which I have seen I now can see no more. . . .

The sunshine is a glorious birth;
But yet I know, where'er I go,
That there hath passed away a glory from the earth.

Now, while the birds thus sing a joyous song,
And while the young lambs bound
As to the tabor's sound,
To me alone there came a quiet thought of grief.
A timely utterance gave that thought relief,
And I again am strong!
The cataracts blow their trumpets from the steep
No more shall grief of mine the season wrong;
I hear the echoes through the mountains throng,
The winds come to me from the fields of sheep,
And all the earth is gay;
Land and sea
Give themselves up to jollity,
And with the heart of May

Doth every beast keep holiday;
Thou child of joy,
Shout round me – let me hear thy shouts, thou happy shepherd-boy!

Wordsworth's child – for which we can read 'the child in all of us' – is thus the embodiment of hope, possessing powers to encourage and help realize optimism in situations where the opposite tendency may be more immediately apparent. Such situations feature a lot in Wordsworth's *Lyrical Ballads*, where on several occasions he draws attention to the lost innocence of childhood occasioned by the temptations of youth (as in, for example, 'Nutting'), or an untimely and premature death (as in 'There was a Boy' and 'Lucy Gray'), an event, considered metaphorically, that illustrates the manner in which youthful promise is too easily thrown off or forgotten about in adulthood (see Blades 2004, pp. 7–42).

The overlap here with Rousseau's image of the child are plain enough, leading me to wonder if Wordsworth had read *Emile*. There is no agreement among scholars on this issue. Barker, for example, is unsure, although she does assert that the poet used Rouseeau's *Social Contract* (published in the same year as *Emile*) in his own arguments against monarchy, aristocracy and primogeniture (Barker 2000, p. 83). On the other hand, in subsequent discussion of the Wordsworths' education of Basil Caroline Montagu (the child of a widowed friend of the family whom they took under their wing from the age of 2), she states that their approach, while it 'may have been determined by the philosophy of Rousseau ... [probably] owed more to [William's] memories of his own happy childhood' (p. 114), about which I will say more in the next chapter.

Barker's uncertainty here reflects accurately what has been concluded generally about the matter. Rosenberg, in a short essay on the educational and Romantic legacy of Rousseau, recounts the variety of opinions on the extent of Wordsworth's debt to him, quoting a string of experts with contrasting attitudes. Thus, one terms Rousseau's influence as 'more powerful perhaps than any other to which Wordsworth was subjected', while another considers the philosopher's effect to be almost non-existent, doubting that 'the poet had any first-hand knowledge of Rousseau', whose *Emile* 'he probably had never even read or heard of' (Rosenberg 1990, pp. 11–12).

My own view is more akin to that of the first of these two experts. For sure, I cannot produce a single shred of evidence to link directly Wordsworth's and Rousseau's views of childhood. But the close analogies between *Emile* and some of the themes of *The Prelude* and *Lyrical Ballads* suggest that the intellectual relationship is too striking to be simply a coincidence. Moreover, why should Wordsworth read and use Rousseau's political arguments in *The Social Contract*, but then choose to ignore his educational ones in *Emile*, which were published at about the same time, and which represent a reworking of the main planks of his whole philosophical outlook.

But this is an argument that need not detain us. For what really matters is what Wordsworth and his fellow Romantics had to say on the subject of childhood, and the education of the child. Returning, then, to the central plot of the present discussion, I want finally to reflect on why I think recalling positively the images of childhood promoted by the Romantics, including Rousseau, can help to illuminate contemporary debates in education.

Lessons from the Romantics about childhood

Beginning with Rousseau, it is no exaggeration to say that *Emile* is one of the most influential works in educational thought. Testimony to the impact of Rousseau's ideas is provided, for example, by such notables as Montessori, Pestalozzi, Froebel and Dewey, not to mention those luminaries of progressive education, Ivan Illich and A.S. Neill, all of whom developed theories of child-centred learning that owe something to the prospectus outlined in *Emile*.

In his critical appreciation of *Emile*, the philosopher of education Richard Peters draws attention to the manner in which Rousseau 'put childhood on the map as a generally accepted entity' (1981, p. 30), placing 'the child at the centre of the educational stage rather than the curriculum or the teacher' (p. 15). In this way, Rousseau anticipated the emphasis currently given in pedagogic theory and practice to pupil-learning rather than teacher-teaching, although there is no suggestion in his work that teachers should abdicate all responsibility for guiding their pupils in particular directions. On the contrary, according to *Emile*, while teachers should never act in an authoritarian manner towards pupils, least of all threaten and order them about, they can, indeed must, exercise proper authority over them from time to time, so as to persuade them in particular that certain things are more worth learning than others. To that extent, to quote Peters again, Rousseau was 'franker and more perceptive' than many of the progressive educators who came after him, and whose ideas they claim are partly based on his.

On the other hand, close reading of some of the analysis and prescriptions found in *Emile* raises eyebrows. Thus, while Rousseau is eloquent in his denunciation of those forms of book-learning that go beyond the experience of the child, his view that children should largely be kept away from reading books altogether until they attain pre-adolescent years is frankly silly. Also, his proposal that the proper upbringing and education of children should obey the dictates of God's providential arrangement of nature, following strictly its alleged rhythms (they must 'learn [their] paces like a saddle-horse, and be shaped in [their] master's tastes like the trees in his garden', rather than the requirements of human inclination) assumes there exists an absolute natural order of things, including a God capable of creating it, which is for many people a highly debatable point. Similarly, it must be an unsubstantiated idealization to insist, as Rousseau did, that mankind has certain innate tendencies, and that rearing and educating children should therefore properly and centrally involve teachers and parents bringing them into harmony with the natural order of things.

So, where does this leave Rousseau and, by inference, the views of both Blake and Wordsworth on childhood and the education of children? And what, if any, should be their lasting legacy for education? While Peters' critique of Rousseau's *Emile* is generally sympathetic, it ends with a back-handed compliment: 'He was a man of great sensitivity ... whose feelings were more highly developed than his judgement' (Peters 1981, p. 31). Similarly, Robert Dearden (whose own work is modelled on the analytic tradition of the philosophy of education which Peters helped to found), commenting on the alleged incoherence of many of the central organizing ideas of progressive theories of education, writes: 'in spite of [their] importance, one searches in vain for an adequate ... elucidation'; they function, he maintains, merely 'as symbolic images, pregnant with meaning and rich in emotional appeal' (1968, p. 24).

I am not sure what to make of these judgements, particularly Peters' assessment of Rousseau's 'highly developed feelings'. What is so wrong with having feelings of a highly developed nature, even when they result in judgements that are less than perfect? Surely there are occasions when many judgements might be all the better for some feeling being behind them, and for them also being sensitively expressed (which is more maybe than can be said for Peters' evaluation of Rousseau's intellectual personality). Also, it strikes me as odd that an analytic philosopher of education such as Dearden should, in any event, be so worried by the fact that some words are 'pregnant with meaning and rich in emotional appeal'. This seems an unnecessary anxiety, not least because that is often what must be the case where educational terms are concerned. As Wittgenstein once wrote, 'meaning is use', and one meaning of certain kinds of words, notably educational ones, is precisely their emotional appeal. This doesn't of course exhaust the meaning of such words, but neither does it necessarily detract from them. So, while I am happy to endorse the suggestion that pedagogic practice should always somehow be significantly based on a form of conceptual coherence of the kind commended by Peters and Dearden, I am convinced that a degree of emotional feeling in the process, of the kind advocated by the Romantics, is also necessary. Indeed, given the highly complex aesthetics of teaching and learning, which make both very difficult to sum up simply, it may not always be possible for a teacher to be fully clear about his or her ideology in the classroom. This is not an excuse for sloppy reasoning; rather it is an appeal to take into account the ethnographic features of that community of practice known as teaching, which makes the effort of making predictions about what is happening in it extremely difficult to sustain without qualification. Interestingly, Rousseau appears to have unintentionally anticipated critics such as Peters and Dearden, observing in one of his letters that he has 'a hundred times in writing made the reflection that it is impossible ... always to give the same meaning to the same words. There is no language rich enough to furnish as many terms, turns, and phrases as our ideas can have modifications' (Rousseau, in Rosenberg 1990, p. 28). This seems about right to me.

As indeed is the challenge that both Blake's and Wordsworth's concepts of childhood hold up to certain rigid ideas about education: ideas that find expression in Stone's first, second and third historic views (outlined earlier), which still exert an influence today. For instance, there are teachers who think that some children whose behaviour is especially obnoxious may need a 'short sharp shock' to bring them round; or that some children are, by virtue of family background, inevitably bound to fail at school; or that the best kind of schoolwork is the sort that requires children to have their empty heads filled up with the teacher's knowledge, which they must memorize and duplicate.

By contrast, Blake's view of the child as 'innocent' and Wordsworth's as 'divine' act to remind all teachers of the special nature of childhood, which both suggest should be viewed as a glorious period in its own right, rather than as a mere preparation ground for adulthood. A version of this reminder of course is equally capable of challenging those conceptions of the educational process that interpret it overly as a preparation for future employment. To that extent, there is a strong liberal education thrust behind Blake's and Wordsworth's advocacy of childhood. Behind it also is the related and important idea of the continuity of the self, which is particularly evident in Wordsworth's scheme. This idea acts to encourage us to think of life as more than the sum of its seeming parts (childhood, adolescence, teenager, young person, early and late middle-ager, senior citizen), entailing instead a distinctive whole, in which learning is not more or less associated with one period of years than any other, but is rather viewed as being lifelong.

Teachers looking for detailed tips of how better to teach will not find much to help them in either Wordsworth's or Blake's poetry. And, as I have indicated, they will also be at a loss to know what to make of some of Rousseau's specific ideas on the subject, though his positive conception of the importance of time-wasting provides a helpful paradoxical corrective to the view, prevalent today, that children in class should be continuously occupied and challenged. Rousseau's views on this subject are worth linking with Blake's – specifically the mood the latter puts into the words of the nurse in his poem in *Songs of Experience*, quoted earlier, telling the children in her care that their 'spring and [their] day are wasted in play'. Rousseau would have challenged directly the nurse's attitude in Blake's poem, for he was all in favour of wasting time: 'Dare I expose the greatest, the most important, the most useful rule of all education? It is not to gain time, but to lose it ... [Don't you] see that using time badly wastes time far more than doing nothing with it?' Of course Rousseau's applauding of time-wasting here derives entirely from his conception of the importance of offering a 'negative education' to children – one in which the natural order of things takes precedence over the teacher's urgings. While no one today would recommend time-wasting as an important axiom of good pedagogy, the idea that children should, on occasion, be allowed in class to control completely the form, content and pace of their learning is surely not so shocking; on the contrary, it may be necessary in order to engage their interest properly, not to mention to provide an excellent means of affirming their projects, which may well contribute to raising their motivational levels.

Although, as I have said, it is not possible to cull from Wordsworth's life and poetry many specific ideas about teaching, they do reveal a curious, anomalous even, turn of ideas and events. Indeed, any enquiring teacher searching through Wordsworth's output will, I predict, be confused by the fact that for a short period he championed a form of teaching and learning, the underpinning philosophy of which runs completely counter to his own inclinations about childhood. Wordsworth's brief support for the so-called 'Madras system' (also known as the 'monitorial scheme' or 'mutual improvement scheme'), for example, which advocated a highly coercive mode of instruction and an associated Gradgrind-like curriculum, is totally at odds with what he believed generally about the importance of children learning from experience. The explanation for this contradiction in attitudes, however, resides in political pragmatism. As Richardson informs us, the Madras system represented to Wordsworth a necessary but unfortunate 'radical cure for England's social ills and political unrest', embodying a form of schooling 'that combined the rudiments of letters with the inculcation of moral and religious truth' (Richardson 1994, p. 95). Wordsworth's was then simultaneously a reformist and a reactionary educational vision, entailing training and teaching to contain the political threat posed by displaced agricultural workers and labourers living in England's new urban settlements, so as to keep them from ignorance but also out of harm's way.

But such political equivocation apart, I want to insist that, looked at as a whole, the Romantics, but Blake and Wordsworth among them in particular, hand down to us a refreshing view of the huge potential of childhood. They offer us especially an image of the child as the personification of hope, and the idea also that the education of children is one of the main ways of realizing optimism in the adult society they will eventually join and help to recreate. In the chapter that follows we shall learn how this vision found representation in the actual schooling of two particular Romantic writers – Hazlitt and Wordsworth – whose 'negative' early education shaped considerably the kind of adults they went on to become.

3

An Education in Nature and Dissent: The Romantics at School

The 'good' teacher

Pedagogical folklore perpetuates a truism about teaching – that the kind of educators teachers become, indeed the very constructions they place upon what it means to be a 'good' teacher, are often significantly based upon positive recollections of teachers with whom they came into contact during their own schooldays. Such memories cut both ways, of course, with some teachers adopting, usually subconsciously, but occasionally explicitly, a teaching style that runs in a direction entirely opposite from the hated one to which they were subjected.

Either way, such influences can be foundational. Alex Moore has gone further, psychoanalysing their effects along lines that suggest a teacher's calling is a highly complex matter, entailing 'the encounter and recontextualization of predispositions and assumptions based on previous experiences of schools and schooling', leavened by 'the imprint and replay of unresolved tensions, uncomfortable roles, and interactive breakdowns in classroom practice and experience' (Moore 2004, p. 23). He argues that role-model teachers rarely offer up to those that follow them representations of 'good' teaching that can straightforwardly be read off from observed behaviours. On the contrary, when such readings take place they are inevitably refracted through other experiences, some very personal, making teaching a profoundly existential occupation, entailing a distinctive, and *continuous*, reconstruction of an inner professional self that finds public expression in particular pedagogical practices.

Notwithstanding the extraordinary intricacies involved here, I want in this chapter to undertake a somewhat speculative, possibly risky, backward–forward reading of some of the known aspects of the early education of two contributors to the Romantic canon – William Hazlitt and William Wordsworth – in order to gauge the extent to which their schoolboy experiences, which were largely affirming, can speak positively

to aspects of the condition of contemporary schooling. I have chosen to
focus on the early schooling of these Romantic writers because the
educational institutions each attended, though both in their way
remarkable and both middle-class in character, were very different from
one another – in Wordsworth's case, a well-established and respected
grammar school; in Hazlitt's, a controversial and publicly pilloried
dissenting academy.

But, before elaborating on all of this, I intend to give some contextual
details of the sort of education available generally during the years
coinciding with the childhoods of Wordsworth and Hazlitt and the other
Romantic writers who feature in this book.

Education in England, 1780–1830

While there was nothing new about the idea of founding charities for
educational purposes, it was only in the last quarter of the eighteenth
century that the question began to be seriously mooted of providing state-
funded mass elementary schooling in England, though it must be stressed
this was envisaged mostly for boys, with ideas for co-education surfacing
less frequently.

Discussion of the need for such provision, however, was by no means
consensual, for there existed at the time serious reservations about the
necessity, legitimacy even, of government being involved in anything
that could be construed as meddling in the private affairs of individuals.
The broad view was rather that the functions of government should be
largely restricted to the defence of the realm and trade regulation and to
keeping order at home. So, while the philosophical radicalism of Locke
during these years buttressed firmly the suggestion that education had a
proper social engineering function, an atomistic view of society, based on
utilitarian individualism, simultaneously led many to object to the idea of
bringing into existence a national system of schooling to facilitate this
process, arguing that to do so would constitute an improper interference
with people's lives.

Thus, in terms that resonate interestingly with Margaret Thatcher's
famous comment that 'there is no such thing as society [only] ...
individual men and women, and ... families' (*Woman's Own*, 31 October
1987), Jeremy Bentham, the earliest historical exponent of utilitarianism,
stated in his introduction to *Principles of Morals and Legislation* (1789) that
'the community is a fictitious body, composed of the individual persons
who are considered, as it were, its members'. This sentiment was widely

held in the late eighteenth century, leading those who advocated it to insist that it was an individual's right and responsibility, and not the state's, to look after his own business, including that of acquiring some education. As Wardle puts it:

> It was conceived to be a man's duty to be responsible for himself and his family, and, although casual assistance by charity or otherwise might be permissible in times of unusual distress, any regular scheme of assistance was thought to be dangerous because it pauperized the recipient and destroyed his sense of independence.
>
> (Wardle 1970, p. 3)

Self-reliance then (as increasingly now) was the main watchword in discussions of welfare.

But there were further aspects to this, each having nothing directly to do with the principle of utility or the maintenance of habits of self-sufficiency. For, even when concessions had been made to the advocates of mass school provision by those instinctively opposed to its introduction, the latter remained anxious about the level and character of the instruction appropriate to the various sections of English society. Did the lower orders engaged in manual and menial labour need to be literate or numerate, let alone have access to more developed skills and areas of knowledge? And what about the likely negative social consequences of providing education for the masses? Might this not contribute to the development of less servile attitudes among the labouring classes? Given such a concern, it is not surprising that ideas on mass education encountered considerable resistance from the wealthier classes, based chiefly on the fear of what an informed and literate populace might do in terms of acting 'above their station'. Would-be mass educators were therefore suspected sometimes of formenting revolution. Accordingly, the general attitude of the governing classes of the time was that a liberal education – one going beyond the 'basics' – should be confined entirely to their own kind, and that elementary education for the masses should be minimal, designed to inculcate religious principles, social obedience and low-level occupational skills. Thus conceived, an elementary education was regarded as one means of stabilizing, if not controlling, the masses.

Such elementary education as was available for the mass of the population in England in the eighteenth century was provided chiefly by the Church or private enterprise supplemented by philanthropy. The fine-grain detail of all of this need not detain us, for it is all set down at a length greater than can be justified here in standard works on the subject (see Simon 1974. In broad-brush terms there was a gradual growth in numbers in England of both private town 'common schools' and the more lowly village 'dame schools' during the second half of the eighteenth century. The former were small-scale and usually held at a teacher's house (often in a damp cellar), where children, up to 40 in number, aged between 5 and 14 years, on payment of a few pennies, received rudimentary instruction in spelling, reading, writing, arithmetic and book-keeping. Village dame schools were similar, though usually co-educational, involving a woman looking after ('minding' for much of the time) local children in her parlour, teaching them to read, knit and sew for whatever their poor parents could afford to pay each week. The significance of these institutions can be gauged by the fact that, in the 1830s, over one-third of all those children receiving some elementary education in Manchester, Salford, Bury, Liverpool and Birmingham were doing so in a common or dame school (Gosden 1969, p. 8). The other two-thirds received rudimentary instruction in a variety of other places, including church schools, subscription charity schools, sunday schools, monitorial schools and a miscellany of endowed schools underwritten by the financial largesse of a local wealthy benefactor.

The education in England of children from relatively well-off, middle-class families, on the other hand, was chiefly through private tuition in the home, followed later by attendance at a boarding or endowed grammar school, sometimes called a 'public' school. By 1818, it is estimated there were about 500 of these schools scattered throughout the country, a select historic few of which were already enjoying an elite status (Westminster, Winchester, Eton, Harrow, Rugby and Charterhouse, for example) due largely to being patronized by wealthy and aristocratic families over several generations. Shelley's alma mater was Eton, while Byron's was Harrow.

So far as numbers were concerned, some of the public schools had more than 400 pupils (Westminster School, for example, had 483 on roll in 1766, 50 of whom were noblemen, noblemen's sons or baronets, while Christ's Hospital School, where Coleridge was educated, had twice this number), but most of the rest were very small, having fewer than 30 pupils, all occupying a single classroom, with instruction conducted by one master and an usher-assistant. The curriculum was classical, based on the teaching of Latin and Greek, with little emphasis on mathematics or science.

Attendance at a prestigious public school such as Eton or Westminster was one of the main routes at the time to a university education in England which, until 1828, could be obtained at only two places – Oxford or Cambridge. The Anglican affiliation of the colleges that made up these two universities meant that teaching positions in them were confined largely to ordained Church of England clergymen. The size of their student intake varied considerably. The number attending Oxford in the eighteenth century was at a particularly low ebb, with no more than 250 freshmen going up annually, compared to 450 matriculating at around the time of the Restoration in 1660, while Cambridge's intake declined even more markedly in the same period. Growing prosperity, coupled with middle-class ambition, however, pushed these numbers significantly upwards as the old century drew to a close and the new one began. Oxford and Cambridge's curriculum, like the one offered in the public schools, concentrated almost exclusively on the classics. This narrow curriculum continued to find favour for as long as a classical education was regarded as a necessary basis for embarking upon a career in the Church or the law.

As professional training grounds, however, Oxford and Cambridge began to face considerable and increasing competition in the late eighteenth century from the so-called dissenting academies. Set up by leading Nonconformists in England, over 70 of these institutions sprang into existence in the 50 years before 1800. Constituting a heterogeneous collection of day and boarding schools, from the genteel to the rough, they operated for varying periods of time in and around London (Cheam, Hoxton, Hackney, Peckham) and in the provinces (Wakefield, York, Daventry, Northampton, Warrington, Manchester). They varied in size – some having 50 or more pupils, others fewer than 20 – with staff numbers equivalently diminutive.

Their relatively small size did not inhibit the dissenting academies' capacity for innovation. This was most evident in what they taught. Their curricula were broad, going well beyond the basics and the classics, offering the first-ever general education featuring modern, scientific and commercial subjects, which were taught, in the best of them, in similar fashion to a university degree. Some in fact were highly progressive, with both the Chelsea and Hackney academies using teaching methods influenced by ideas gleaned from Rousseau's *Emile* (see Simon 1974, pp. 56–62; Clarke 1940, p. 16). Such progressiveness in teaching methods, however, was the exception rather than the rule. For children from every social class, attending any type of school in the 1700s, would have been expected to learn mostly in silence, via recitation, under a pedagogic regime in which strict discipline was maintained, frequently through the use of severe sanctions, including corporal punishment. Dr Johnson was therefore accurate when, in his famous *Dictionary* (first issued in 1755), he defined a 'school' as a 'house of discipline and instruction', and tellingly in that sequence of words.

Mention of the Warrington and Hackney Dissenting Academies highlights the significant personality of Joseph Priestley, who, besides being an eminent scientist of his day, was a keen public advocate of educational reform at the turn of the eighteenth century, as well as a one-time tutor in both institutions, and a teacher for a short time of William Hazlitt. Priestley, who was a conspicuous example of the type of radical-rationalist and broadly educated intellectual that the Warrington and Hackney academies were partly set up to create, called for a more liberal view of education, entailing major changes to the sort of curriculum on offer in the grammar schools of his time. Besides wanting students to learn new subjects, such as history, economic and commercial geography and chemistry, Priestley had equally strong views about methods of teaching, which he thought should encourage pupil participation in the form of discussion in class and the asking of questions, leading pupils to express their own points of view, his object being 'to train them, without fear to look for every species of ill-usage in a good cause' (Maclean 1943, p. 64).

Despite the radicalism exhibited in his appeals for curricular and pedagogical reform, Priestley was adamantly opposed to education becoming a function of the state, chiefly because he believed that a government-mandated system of schooling for everyone would promote uniformity of thought and belief – an argument that has a contemporary feel to it. To be sure it fits also, as we saw earlier, with the views of other well-educated people of the time, finding expression in some of Hazlitt's writings, though not Wordsworth's, the latter being less enthusiastic about the benefits of education made available to everyone in the land. It is to a consideration of the kind of schooling from which he derived such advantage that I now turn, but not without first looking at Hazlitt's brief experience of being formally educated.

Hazlitt's days at New College, Hackney

Hazlitt was 15 years old when, in the summer of 1793, he first became a pupil at the dissenting academy in Hackney, which was then in its sixth year of existence. New College, to give it its official name, was housed at the time in a large mansion, standing in 15 acres of grounds, accommodating pupils of all Christian denominations, despite its status as a training ground for Unitarian clergymen. Hackney's pupils preparing to enter the ministry followed a course lasting five years; lay pupils underwent a shorter, three-year programme of study.

In its first year the college enrolled a mere 14 pupils, all of whom were residential. It is not clear how many pupils were attending the college when Hazlitt joined it, though given that six tutors worked there in 1793, one can assume they were responsible for the education of a larger number, possibly up to 30. One of these tutors, Dr Price, defined the primary aim of Hackney as 'promoting such a spirit of inquiry and candour, as shall form worthy citizens for the state, and useful ministers for the church' (Maclean 1943, p. 63). Elsewhere, writing in the college prospectus in 1787, he stated that

the best education ... [is one which] ... impresses the heart with the love of virtue, and communicates the most expanded and ardent benevolence; which gives the deepest consciousness of the fallibility of the human understanding, and preserves us from vile dogmatism so prevalent in the world; which makes men diffident and modest, attentive to evidence, capable of proportioning their assent to the degree of it, quick in discerning it, and determined to follow it; which in short, instead of producing acute casuists, conceited pedants, or furious polemics, produces fair enquirers.

(Grayling 2000, p. 32)

Hackney's aim to produce 'fair enquirers' found explicit expression in the ambitious curriculum it offered, which included a wide range of subjects, far superior to that found in any contemporary grammar or public school. Hazlitt, in fact, was spoilt for choice, being able to study not only the subjects that made up the then staple diet of a classical education, but also ancient and modern geography, universal grammar, rhetoric and composition, chronology, civil and ecclesiastical history, the principles of law and government, mathematics, astronomy, natural and experimental physics and chemistry, logic, metaphysics, ethics, natural and revealed religion, theology, critical lectures on the scriptures, and elocution. For additional payment (the college's basic fee was £60 per annum), he could also receive tuition in French and other modern languages, as well as in drawing.

The kind of curriculum offered by New College, Hackney, although not repeated throughout the dissenting academies movement, was not typical of it. Thus the four-year course offered by Northampton Academy, an institution founded more than 50 years before New College, included many similar subjects, as well as others not so familiar, such as celestial mechanics, natural and experimental philosophy, orations and mythology. Raymond Williams maintained that the dissenting academies had 'worked out and put into practice a new definition of the content of a general education' (Williams 1965, p. 154), which anticipated in some aspects the sort of academic curriculum which today is taken largely for granted.

It was not just Hackney's curriculum that set it apart as a liberal seat of learning. As one would expect, given the presence of Joseph Priestley on its staff, whose pedagogical theories encouraged student participation and debate, the college was daringly experimental in other ways too, with 'freedom of expression' being central to its philosophy of teaching and learning. This philosophy encouraged a form of radical intellectualism among pupils, who were encouraged by their tutors and guest lecturers (which included Tom Paine) to challenge generally accepted opinion. This predictably offended that section of England's governing class at which much of this criticism was directed. So, while the college was undoubtedly at the cutting edge of education in late-eighteenth-century England, it managed to bring down upon itself considerable opprobrium from among the less liberally inclined, who denounced it as a hotbed of sedition. Worse still, there is evidence that the college was suffering some internal indiscipline at around the time Hazlitt began his studies there, some of which concerned allegations of moral laxity involving a section of its boarders. As Maclean observes,

> it is difficult to avoid the conclusion that ... the students [at Hackney] needed the rein rather than the spur, that they were too full of crude life for those set in authority over them, that they were inclined to intervene mischievously in matters in which they had no power to intervene usefully, and that the tolerant idealism and generous liberalism of the founders were being abused rather than used, to an extent that imperiled the usefulness and came near to endangering the existence of the college.
>
> (Maclean 1943, p. 65)

Hazlitt tells us absolutely nothing about this in his first letters home, which are full of comments about how much he is missing his family and news of the studies he is embarking upon (Sikes 1978, pp. 60–70). Thus it is difficult to judge with any certainty if the antics of some pupils at the college had any influence on the decision to withdraw him from its roll after only two years, though one can speculate that his father – a Unitarian minister – would have taken unkindly to reports of immorality, and so might not have wished his son to remain at the college. Another factor that may well have encouraged Hazlitt senior to withdraw his son prematurely was the knowledge that William seemed to have lost the vocation he once had to become a clergyman – the reason why his family sent him to the college in the first place. There may also have been a financial problem, despite William's scholarship status.

Either way, given the brevity of Hazlitt's time at the college, there is not much to work with in terms of gauging its impact on him, although one incident is very instructive, both in terms of revealing much about Hackney's stance on independent learning and about William's already highly developed independence of thought and spirit. The incident is well known, and reported in most of the biographies. Hazlitt's classics teacher, John Corrie, set him the task of writing within a week an essay on a certain theme. When Corrie asked Hazlitt for his essay, Hazlitt told him that it had not been written. Corrie dismissed Hazlitt, demanding that he complete the task within the hour. Hazlitt dithered, being preoccupied with another, more pressing, demand on his time, leading him again to fail to complete the set work. He was confronted by Corrie who asked him in a gentle but sarcastic way if he had ever written anything in his life. Hazlitt replied that he most certainly had, producing the manuscript on which he has been working on instead – a still incomplete 'Essay on Laws'. Instead of venting further irritation on the wayward Hazlitt, Corrie encouraged him to go away and finish the law essay, rather than the work originally set.

This story is revealing in two obvious ways: first, it tells us a lot about the college's educational priorities, as mediated through Corrie's actions, which centre on seeking to meet the needs of students, even sometimes at the expense of tutors' expectations; and, second, it tells us about the young Hazlitt's ambitions. For while Hazlitt is undoubtedly happy for much of the time to attend satisfactorily to the routine work demanded of him at Hackney; but he has an educational agenda of his own, from which he is resolved ultimately not to be distracted by mere book-learning. There is, then, as revealed in this short anecdote, a complete synergy of interest between college and student: something very rare in most other people's education at that time, and arguably since.

Besides this story, we also know that Hazlitt did well at Hackney, despite over-studying, often busily engaging himself in his own private work on top of that prescribed by his tutors. Maclean writes:

[Hazlitt's] day begins at seven in the morning, and goes on, with little relaxation except an hour and a half walking, until seven o'clock at night. It is difficult to see ... when he takes time to eat and drink ... Preparation for his lectures takes up much of his time. In addition, there is his writing; and he spends the last hour and a half of the day, from half-past nine until eleven, which is supposed to be his bedtime, reading.

(Maclean 1943, p. 72)

By any estimate, this is a long school day, and all the more so given the relatively junior age of the person undertaking it, for Hazlitt was barely into his mid-teenage years when a pupil at Hackney.

The New College at Hackney, although small in size, and in some ways, at times, undisciplined, was probably the only educational establishment of its day in which the young Hazlitt could have thrived, and in which he would have chosen freely to work so hard both at his own studies and at those set down by his tutors. His gains were great. For not only did Hazlitt have access at Hackney to a form of general education unheard of outside of the dissenting academies movement, including the two universities of his time, but also the opportunity to pursue to the limit his own private interests and passions, including the development of his political attitudes, which were already radical and oppositional. The college also had a large library, which supplemented the books in his father's house. He borrowed and read voraciously, obsessively even. In addition, at Hackney, Hazlitt came into contact with tutors who were, all of them, if not people of genius, at least people of significant intellectual mark. The freedom of thought encouraged by these tutors, even if it sometimes endangered the college's reputation and very existence, was the best thing in the world for a mind like Hazlitt's. All he needed was to be left to develop without too much interference from those in authority, and it seems he enjoyed and took full advantage of this freedom. Hackney suited well his dissenting genius.

Hackney also began to establish in his mind several attitudes about education: what it is for and of what it should consist. As I previously indicated, like many of his intellectual peers, Hazlitt doubted the need for a free national education system designed to provide the labouring classes with schooling in the 'basics' of learning how to read, write and count. In his case, this was partly because he saw such an education as far too limiting a vision, but more significantly because he did not hold out much hope of it as a reforming possibility for the masses.

According to Hazlitt, the main stuff of a real education comes not from being schooled, but from a combination of reading and observation, neither complete without the other, with both being the lifelong responsibility of each of us. True, Hazlitt commends, the importance of having a narrow formal grounding in the classics which might seem to be the antithesis of his conception of a 'real' education. But this would be to misunderstand his position. For Hazlitt's admiration of a classical education was largely due to what he saw as its lack of faddishness, and its associated celebration of a way of thinking that, crucially for him, had an established rather than ephemeral value ('it fixes our thoughts on the remote and permanent, instead of narrow and fleeting objects' (Wu, 1998, 2, p. 8). When Hazlitt does criticize a classical education, it is to draw attention to the totally inadequate version of it provided by the universities of his time, which he considered far too narrowly book-based and insufficiently linked with experience, making it a poor substitute for the sort of general education which he judged to be the hallmark of a genuinely thoughtful and educated personality. As he jokingly puts it:

> I do not wish to speak against a classical education; it refines and softens, I grant ... But surely it often gives a false estimate of men and things. Everyone brought up in colleges, and drugged with Latin and Greek for a number of years, firmly believes *that there have been about five people in the world, and that they are dead* ... [These] the classical standard turns shadows into realities and realities into shadows'.

Wordsworth's schooling at Hawkshead

Hazlitt would surely have approved of the humane way in which the classics were taught at Hawkshead Grammar School – the school which Wordsworth attended for five years from 1779. For the young Wordsworth – he was just 9 when he first joined the school – was not 'drugged' there to understand, first, Virgil and Ovid, and then Homer and Cicero (see Gill 1989, p. 27). Rather he was helped to appreciate their beauty through being introduced to them in a familiar fashion that eschewed wearisome rote-learning and repetitious exercises in verse composition. The fact that Wordsworth continued to educate himself in the classics long after leaving Hawkshead, delighting in classical poetry throughout his adult life, must be attributed, to some degree, to early teaching of rare quality. Certainly, if we accept as true the very positive account Wordsworth provides of his childhood in *The Prelude*, we must conclude that his schooldays at Hawkshead were extremely happy ones. They were also completed in a school surrounded by a natural environment whose beauty both captivated and tutored his aesthetic judgement for the better.

The southern Cumbrian village of Hawkshead, site of Wordsworth's grammar school, lies high up in the hills between the great lakes of Windermere and Coniston, at the northernmost end of Esthwaite Water. It was a lovely setting then; it is still lovely today. The school itself, positioned just inside the village churchyard, was housed in a two-storey whitewashed stone building, little more than the size of a large cottage. The contrast with Hazlitt's New College could not have been greater, for the latter was accommodated on a much grander scale in a fairly urban locality. Into the much smaller building that was Hawkshead Grammar School were crammed somewhere in the region of a hundred pupils. Their studies, which began early in the morning and ended late in the afternoon, were conducted in a single large rectangular schoolroom. At one end of this room, on a dais and next to a huge fireplace, stood the master's desk; at the other end was the desk of the usher (his assistant). Wordsworth would have sat, with all the other pupils, on one of several benches that stood between these two teachers, working at a single simple ledge which stood in for a desk. As classrooms go, and by the standards of today, Wordsworth's was not an especially attractive one. It is a measure of the high quality of the teaching he enjoyed in it that this fact compromised not one bit the progress he made.

Wordsworth was a clever and interested pupil, often being left by his teachers to his own devices to read whatever books he liked. Much of his education was conducted informally out-of-doors, where with other schoolboys he explored the countryside all about the school. When Wordsworth was taught formally in class, he was given not only excellent instruction in the classics and English grammar and composition, but also – and this was a noted specialism of Hawkshead – mathematics and science, both of which captured his imagination to a high degree, complementing and feeding his emerging literary inclinations.

But it was mostly the extra and exceptional encouragement Wordsworth received from two of the school's masters – first, William Taylor (until his death in 1786) and then Thomas Bowman, his successor – that made all the difference to his education. Both were significant influences on him. According to a contemporary, Taylor had 'extensive learning, a sound judgment, a modest demeanour and unblemished morals' (Marples 1967, p. 22). A clergyman and Fellow of Emmanuel College, Cambridge, he was an enthusiastic teacher, meeting his pupils at play as well as at work, which no doubt shocked orthodox opinion. Taylor, a passionate lover of poetry, passed on his enthusiasm for literature to Wordsworth. Thomas Bowman, also a clergyman and a graduate of Cambridge University, did the same, purchasing on a monthly basis the latest 'best' books, many of them poetry collections, which he installed in a growing Hawkshead school library, from which Wordsworth borrowed on a regular basis. It was Taylor, however, who first encouraged Wordsworth to write poetry of his own, a fact he acknowledges in *The Prelude*, where he writes: 'The kind hope/Which he [Taylor] had formed when I sat at his command/Began to spin, at first, my toilsome songs' (Book 10, 512–14). Earlier in *The Prelude*, in Book 5, Wordsworth tells us that he was about 13 years old, or in his final year at Hawkshead,

> ... when first
> My ears began to open to the charm
> Of words in tuneful order, found them sweet
> For *their own sakes* – a passion and a power –
> And phrases pleased me, chosen for delight,
> For pomp, or love.
>
> (*The Prelude*, Book 5, 576–81)

Of course, Wordsworth's memory here could be faulty, except that in another place, and at another time, directly in his 1843 note to his poem 'An Evening Walk', he quotes a particular image confirming that his first efforts at verse composition overlapped with his time at Hawkshead Grammar:

> I recollect distinctively the very spot where this first struck me. It was in the way between Hawkshead and Ambleside, and gave me extreme pleasure. The moment was very important in my poetical history, for I date from it my consciousness of the infinite variety of natural appearances which had been unnoticed by the poets of any age or country, so far as I was acquainted with them: and I made a resolution to supply in some degree of deficiency. I could not have been at that time above fourteen years of age.
>
> (Barker 2000, p. 39)

Notwithstanding the encouragement and influence of his teachers at Hawkshead, the greatest stimulation to Wordsworth's youthful genius was the beauty of his environment. Like 'The Boy of Winander' (*The Prelude*,

Book 5), Wordsworth's 'negative education' at Hawkshead Grammar School mostly took place in natural settings – 'Beneath the trees or by the glimmering lake' – where, his poetry tells us, he skilfully cups his hands to blow 'mimic hootings to the silent owls', which are tricked into answering and revealing their presence. Such spontaneous moments of self-abandonment allowed nature to enter directly and unconsciously into Wordsworth's very being, even at such a young age:

> And they would shout
> Across the watery vale, and shout again,
> Responsive to his call, – with quivering peals
> And long halloos, and screams, and echoes loud
> Redoubled and redoubled; concourse wild
> Of jocund din! And, when there came a pause
> Of silence such as baffled his best skill:
> Then, sometimes, in that silence, while he hung
> Listening, a gentle shock of mild surprise
> Has carried far into his heart the voice
> Of mountain torrents; or the visible scene
> Would enter unawares into his mind
> With all its solemn imagery, its rocks,
> Its woods, and that uncertain heaven received
> Into the bosom of the steady lake.
>
> (*The Prelude*, Book 5, 399–413)

This 'shock of mild surprise', as Wordsworth describes it here in *The Prelude*, arose from him suddenly becoming aware of his surroundings. In old age, reflecting on the way in which his mind as a child could become possessed with images of nature, and to such a degree that they seemed to take him over completely, Wordsworth says:

> I was often unable to think of external things as having external existence, and I communed with all that I saw as something not apart from me, but inherent, in my own immaterial nature. Many times while going to school have I grasped at a wall or tree to recall myself from this abyss of idealism to the reality.
>
> (Gill 1989, p. 33, footnote)

This contact with the grandeur and beauty of the natural world, and the self-forgetfulness in which the imagination is given full scope to accept what reason cannot grasp, is a central dictum of *The Prelude*, and indeed of

Wordsworth's poetry in general. So is the importance he gives to the role of book-based learning, and the reading of fantastic stories of magic and adventure in particular, which are seen by him as second only to nature in developing a child's imagination and understanding:

> O give us once again the wishing cap
> Of Fortunatus, and the invisible coat
> Of Jack the Giant-Killer, Robin Hood
> And Sabra in the forest with Saint George!
> The child, whose love is here, at least doth reap
> One precious gain, that he forgets himself.
>   (*The Prelude*, Book 5, 341–6)

Wordsworth believed strongly that reading such tales helped children to escape the limitations of overly rational conceptions of the world of experience:

> Ye dreamers, then,
> Forgers of daring tales! We bless you then,
> Imposters, drivellers, dotards as the ape
> Philosophy will call you: then we feel
> With what, and how great might ye are in league,
> Who make our wish, our power, our thought a deed
> An empire, a possession, – ye whom time
> And seasons serve; all Faculties:– to whom
> Earth crouches, the elements are potter's clay,
> Space like a heaven filled up with northern lights,
> Here, nowhere, there, and everywhere at once.
>   (Book 5, 523–33)

But it is 'nature', and the child's direct experience of it, that affords the best education in Wordsworth's scheme, which is why, like Hazlitt, he distrusted mere book-learning and the pedantry that often accompanies it. He opposed also all systems of thought that subdivided knowledge into narrow specialisms, particularly when this resulted in the creation of an artificial barrier between the learner and a direct engagement with the world of nature:

> Sweet is the lore which Nature brings;
> Our meddling intellect
> Misshapes the beauteous forms of things:

We murder to dissect.
        ('The Tables Turned', 25–8, in Gill 1984, p. 131)

Wordsworth never denied that book-learning is an important aspect of becoming an educated person. Quite the opposite. His own education included a great deal of it, for which he was always grateful. The point is rather that Wordsworth did not consider this to be sufficient. Nature, mediated by a 'wiser Spirit' than that provided by the authors of books (by which, of course, is meant the providence of God), is the essential ingredient – for, ultimately, there can be, Wordsworth tells us repeatedly, no knowledge without it:

> These mighty workmen of our later age
> Who with a broad highway have overbridged
> The forward chaos of futurity,
> Tam'd to their bidding; they who have the art
> To manage books, and things, and make them work
> Gently on infant minds, as does the sun
> Upon a flower; the Tutors of our Youth
> The Guides, the wardens of our faculties ...
> Sages, who in their prescience would control
> All accidents, and to the very road
> Which they have fashion'd would confine us down,
> Like engines, when they will be taught
> That in the unreasoning progress of the world
> A wiser Spirit is at work for us,
> A better eye than theirs, more prodigal
> Of Blessings, and more studious of our good,
> Even in what seem our most unfruitful hours?
>   (*The Prelude*, Book 5, 370–88)

Lessons from the Romantics at school

For Wordsworth, the power of poetry resides in its extraordinary and superior capacity to express 'the most valuable object of all writing ... the great and universal passions of men ... and the entire world of nature'. Hazlitt thought much the same. In a lecture given at the Surrey Institution in 1818, he defined poetry as 'the universal language which the heart holds with nature and itself ... [I]t is the stuff of which our life is made ... for all that is worth remembering in life is the poetry of it' (Wu

1998, 2, p. 165). Wordsworth, more than Hazlitt, however, appreciated the educational implications that follow from their equally high estimations of the significance of the poetic imagination. In Wordsworth's mind's-eye, teaching is an inevitable and inescapable aspect of being a poet. So, while a teacher need not be a poet, for Wordsworth, all poets must be teachers.

But what kind of teacher should the poet seek to be? And what sort of philosophy of education should inform a poet's pedagogic practice? Are there any indications from Wordsworth's and Hazlitt's schooldays, and their subsequent reflections on them, that point up answers to such questions – answers from which today's teachers (most of whom are not poets) might learn? Of course I think there are – indeed I wouldn't be writing this book if I thought otherwise. However, in identifying them, I need to be honest about the extent to which my backward–forward reading of the significance of Wordsworth's time at Hawkshead and Hazlitt's at Hackney is refracted through attitudes I already hold about what counts as a 'good' education and 'good' teaching, including positive experiences of my own of being schooled and educated that incline me to embrace particular educational attitudes rather than others. Some critics, knowing this, might argue, therefore that what I am about to do is essentially an exercise in trawling through the schooldays of Wordsworth and Hazlitt in order to locate supporting evidence for my own prejudices about education. On the other hand, a more generous appreciation of what is about to happen, and the one I naturally prefer, highlights the manner in which the attitudes of these particular Romantics about education serve as important *reminders* of progressive ways of thinking about teaching and learning that have largely been lost sight of at the current juncture, but which deserve to receive renewed attention.

The idea of a 'negative' education is one such attitude. We encountered it first in Rousseau's *Emile*; we see it now writ large in the schooling of both Wordsworth and Hazlitt. For Hazlitt, it finds expression in the actions of his classical teacher, John Corrie, who encouraged him to work at what he found most interesting, rather than spend time on specific set exercises. For Wordsworth, it takes the form of Mr Taylor, who inspired him to read widely and to exercise his imagination. Of course there is a danger here of allowing students to pursue their own interests at the expense of what may formally and justifiably be required of them. But maybe the bigger danger today, when curriculum prescription and the meeting of associated targets chiefly command teachers' attention, is that insufficient time is given over to encouraging students to learn outside the syllabus, and in a manner of their own choosing. The Romantics remind us of the need for more, not less, of this approach, including the importance of surprise in teaching and learning. Allowing oneself as a teacher to be diverted positively from a pre-planned course of action, as a result of an unanticipated insight or intervention, seems to me to be a necessary condition of teaching well, and encouraging pupils to think and act independently is one way of fostering their creative and imaginative capacities.

The Romantics also call to mind the value of a general education, from which both Wordsworth and Hazlitt clearly benefited enormously. While the teaching and learning of subjects is always important, it is Wordsworth in particular who stresses the importance of studying them in an integrated way so as to make full and comprehensive sense of experience. Because Wordsworth abhorred all forms of subject-centredness, he was hostile to attempts to drive artificial barriers between complementary intellectual pursuits. A scholar, today, that exemplifies this attitude well is the sociologist Zygmunt Bauman, who insists that there is 'little substance to the academic divisions apart from such necessities as arise from a mixture of bureaucratic and market considerations'. And, more fundamentally, in the course of reflecting on his lifetime's work as a social theorist, Bauman states:

> experience, unlike the university building, is not divided into departments, let alone tightly sealed departments. Academics may refuse or neglect to read their next floor neighbour's work and so carry unscathed the conviction of their own separate identity, but this cannot be said of human experience, in which the sociological, the political, the economic, the philosophical, the psychological, the historical, the poetic and what not are blended to the extent that no single ingredient can salvage its substance or identity in case of separation.
>
> (Bauman and Tester 2001, pp. 39–40)

This is a 'truth' that both Hazlitt and Wordsworth recognized in their own time, and which we too easily forget in our own.

Despite each being bookish autodidacts, Wordsworth and Hazlitt saw through the limitations of an education in which reading for its own sake was elevated to an importance it neither warranted nor could bear. To be sure, Hazlitt was more than once minded in his life to think that nothing existed in the world to compare with the importance of reading books; and Wordsworth was equally convinced of their value. But neither was convinced that this was enough. On the contrary, they both believed passionately in the need to relate book knowledge to experience. As Hazlitt put it, shortly before his death: 'the world itself is a volume larger than all the libraries in it' (Baker 1962, p. 121). Like Wordsworth, he never saw books as a substitute for life. Indeed, both of them refused to see schooling as constituting the whole of a person's education, viewing it rather as just one part of it. Being educated may require schooling, consisting of much book-learning, but neither is of any use, each of these Romantics teaches us, if it fails to connect with life. Nor, they tell us with equal fervour, and as we are about to find out in the next chapter, is it of any value without love.

4

Education and Romantic Love: Passion and Gusto in Pedagogy

It is in the nature of love to discern Good, and the best love is in some part ... a love of what is Good.

(*Iris Murdoch*, The Sovereignty of Good)

It is impossible to teach without the courage to love.

(*Paulo Freire*)

Learning and loving

Despite it being commonplace to hear teachers say they love their work and their pupils, most surveys of key concepts in education do not include an entry for the word 'love'. Nor does 'love' feature much in academic books and articles about teaching and learning. This greatly surprises me. Love, after all, is at the summit of our moral vocabulary, while education is a profoundly ethical activity, concerned with enabling individuals to pursue worthwhile lives, using pedagogic means that are appreciative and beneficent. The overlaps seem obvious to me. So, why aren't they equally apparent to other educationalists?

I suspect that one reason why the link between these two ideas is insufficiently acknowledged connects with the age-long antipathy between reasoned judgement and emotional expression. This aversion realizes a clash of discourses that inhibits most educational commentators from writing the words 'love' and 'pedagogy' in the same sentence, other than by way of offering a health warning to teachers to 'keep their distance' from pupils, so as to preserve untouched what D.H. Lawrence once referred to as a stretch of 'holy ground' which he said should always exist between teacher and taught.

There are, I need quickly to say, a few significant exceptions to this tendency, such as Daniel Liston's and Jim Garrison's recently issued collection, *Teaching, Learning and Loving* (2004), which bravely 'reasserts and re-inserts the passions, the loves, the emotions back into education', speaking 'loudly in public about what many think should only be spoken about softly in private' (pp. 1–2). For these writers love is integral to good pedagogy – 'it is a creative, critical, and disruptive force' in education, possessing the capacity 'to fuel our intent to act against the barriers that block an abundant and engaged approach to teaching and learning' (p. 3). Didier Maleuvre's (2005) conception of aesthetic education similarly illustrates how teaching and learning, in his case about art and literature, have the power not just to train critical thinking, but to awaken the more tender faculties of the mind, kindling generosity, kindness and love. George Steiner's sustained reflection on the subtle interplay of power, trust and passions in the most profound sorts of pedagogy reminds us equally of the loving exultation which accompanies good teaching, irrespective of the subject matter involved: 'To teach seriously is to lay hands on what is most vital in a human being. It is to seek access to the quick and the innermost of a child's ... integrity' (2003, p. 18). Parallel insights are found in Daniel Cho's (2005) claim that love not only has a place within pedagogy, but is necessary for it. Jim Garrison's reconstruction of Dewey's philosophy of education says much the same, concluding that 'teaching success depends upon [teachers'] wisdom about the ways of love' (1997, p. 1). That is my view too, though one that is differently supported, as will become apparent in the course of this chapter.

My immediate starting point, however, is not any direct reflection about teaching and learning, but rather discussion of the indirect educational insights to be derived from studying how love is treated by the Romantic writers that feature in this book. My assumption is that certain aspects of what they say about it are worth drawing into analyses of how adequately to define and practise the art of teaching, including how such teaching can best promote effective learning. Indeed, my attitude is stronger than this, since I consider the concept of Romantic love to be of a kind that anticipates the very essence of good pedagogy.

Its pedagogical importance apart, love is at the epicentre of how the Romantics thought about and conceived of their aesthetic and intellectual contribution. For, despite what is more often than not differently assumed, there are fewer matters of greater importance to most of them than the subject of love. The 'Big Six' poets, to be sure, are better known as poets of rebellion and poets of the imagination. But central to all of them, and also to Hazlitt, in one way or another, is a preoccupation with love – whether of humankind, or of art, or of nature. It is love in fact that makes possible that sublimity or connectedness which is the goal of all of them.

For Wordsworth, there are the 'beauteous forms' of the Wye Valley that move him to a 'far deeper zeal of holier love' (*Tintern Abbey*, 25, 55). Similarly, for Coleridge, as I will emphasize later, love is an instinctive movement of human nature, the affirmation of which represents the completeness of one's self: 'The first lesson that innocent childhood afforded me is that it is an instinct of my nature to pass out of myself, and to exist (for) others' (*Notebooks*). On another occasion, in 1810, in his poem 'The Visionary Hope', Coleridge defines 'Love's despair' as 'Hope's pining ghost! For this one hope he makes his hourly moan, He wishes and can wish for thee alone!' Earlier, in 1799, writing in similar vein, he says:

> All thoughts, all passions, all delights
> Whatever stirs this mortal flame
> All are but ministers of Love
> And feed his sacred flame. ('Love' in Richards 1978, p. 165)

For Hazlitt also it is the failure of love that is the greatest obstacle to a fulfilled life. He probably knew this more than most (see Cook 2007). For, as is well known, Hazlitt's emotional life did not realize his own hopes. His broken marriage and, most striking, crazed courtship of his landlord's daughter, Sarah Walker, all point instead to a failure on his part to live up to the lofty ideals he believed in, some of which find tragic expression in his deeply troubling 'book of love', the shockingly confessional *Liber Amoris*.

Yet, for all that, Hazlitt lived much of his life, as did most of the 'Big Six' poets who were his contemporaries, surrounded by love, both given and received. In the case of some of the poets, it is clear they gave of themselves and got back in return much affection and support. Coleridge, for example, writing in 1809, speaks of his 'twelve years intercommunion with Wordsworth' (*Collected Letters*). Shelley too brought out intense devotion in others, such that Byron exclaimed on at least four occasions that no one in his experience had equalled him in personality and style of life. Even Hazlitt, who managed ultimately to make enemies of both Wordsworth and Coleridge, was able to be magnanimous in his withering criticisms of their altered political views and literary attitudes (see his sometimes scathing profiles of each of them in *The Spirit of the Age*), though it has to be said neither of them easily forgave him for what they judged to be his intemperate written assessments of their careers which he thought had failed miserably to live up to early promise. Hazlitt, on the other hand, probably thought he was doing them each a favour, offering, if not directly 'in love', at least 'in kindliness', negative opinions of their work and personalities in order to help them to escape the mediocrity into which he believed both had descended, and which he consequently thought reflected poorly on their different geniuses. This, by the way, would be typical of Hazlitt, since he always found it difficult to bear individuals who did not seek continuously to make the most of their abilities. Looked at in this way, Hazlitt was seemingly cruel to Coleridge and Wordsworth, not in order to harm either personally, for he admired each greatly, but rather to assist them to improve and go on to fulfil the high expectations he still had of them and their work.

The nature of love

Anyone even vaguely familiar with the philosophical literature on love will have recognized that different conceptions of its nature have been articulated and reflected in what I have written so far. For the sake of greater clarity, I shall identify what these are. Later on, I shall discuss certain contemporary sociological theories about the nature of love which draw attention less to its significance as a principle of living and more to its fragility in modern societies. For now, though, I will concentrate on Western historical notions of love.

The way the Romantics thought and wrote about love – and the way we mostly think about and experience it today – exists chiefly at the intersection of a set of traditions which derive, initially, from Plato, then subsequently from Aristotle, and finally from early Christian theology. Additionally, the Romantics' conception of love, like that possessed by the rest of us, has its origins in an eighteenth-century British philosophical tradition associated with the empiricism of David Hume that lays great stress on the role feelings should play in obtaining knowledge of the world.

I will get to Hume in due course. Meanwhile, the first tradition listed here, encapsulated in the notion of *eros*, concentrates on love as a form of passionate yearning; the second, manifest in the idea of *philia*, entails a fondness and appreciation of the other, incorporating, in addition to friendship, loyalties to family and to community; and the third, gathered up into the term *agape*, invites us to a charitable notion of love, one which is freely given to all, irrespective of their evident failings and inadequacies, and the necessity of receiving anything in return. Without wanting to diminish the tensions that exist between these three conceptions of love, there are many points at which, in the course of actual experience, they work in harmony in significant ways. Certainly this is true in the educational context, where teachers may simultaneously yearn passionately to succeed in their work and derive extraordinary satisfaction from doing it well (*eros*), while maintaining a strong commitment to the school in which they are employed and to the pupils they teach (*philia*), respecting unequivocally the right of all of them, irrespective of background and ability, to receive the fullest possible education (*agape*). These overlaps, however, at the level both of teachers' actions and thoughts and of people's feelings and behaviour generally are more easily understood if we look more carefully at the specific traditions about love which lie behind them.

Eros refers to that aspect of love which gives most weight to an intense longing for something. While *eros* is often interpreted as sexual craving, this is only a minor part of the story. In Plato's writings, notably in his *Symposium*, it is conceived as a common desire that earnestly seeks out the particular beauty of an individual person, thing or image in order to anticipate the true beauty that exists only in the world of forms or ideas. Reciprocity accordingly is not necessary to this view of love, for the desire, which is *eros*, is for the object of beauty alone, and not for the company of other people, least of all for shared values and pursuits. On the other hand, Plato inaugurates the idea that while *eros* is undeniably a primordial power, giving rise to heightened desires which may overwhelm us, it is amenable to human intention and action since it is capable of being tutored in ways that foster increased discrimination and refinement. The *Symposium* in fact is Plato's effort partly to explicate how the capacities that constitute *eros* may be channelled in ways that render human life happier and more meaningful. Indeed, Plato's insights here represent an original *education of desire*, in the course of which our primitive passions are converted and humanized through an ethic of questioning, which enables us to become lovers of wisdom, which allows us to anticipate true beauty, including the Good.

Whereas *eros* represents a one-way relationship in which we fall in love with what gives us access to what is beautiful and Good, *philia*, as Aristotle explains in the *Nicomachean Ethics*, is a mutual act in which both partners recognize each other's goodwill, seeking to do what is right, not for one's own sake, but for the other's. As Armstrong observes, *philia* 'entails a significant shift in the ordinary pattern of motivation' (2003, p. 109), in the course of which people do not simply (as in the case of *eros*) act according to a vision of self-interest, but rather in ways that promote the good of other people. This profound modification in sensibility connects love with friendship, and each with kindness, making the good person a lover of others as well as a lover of self, because he is related to his friend as to himself: 'in friendship and in love another person comes to be a "second self" – meaning that concern with what is good for them directs our actions just as readily as concern with what is good for us' (Armstrong 2003, p. 109).

This linking of love with friendship finds vivid representation in Sandor Marai's elegiac novel *Embers*. There we read of two old men – Henrik and Konrad – meeting after a long gap, sitting down to a final dinner together, during which they talk of old passions, exploring intensely the nature of their early friendship which a past event has radically fractured and interrupted:

> Friendship [says Henrik] is the most powerful bond in life and consequently the rarest. What is its basis? ... Sympathy? A hollow, empty word, too weak to express the idea that in the worst of times two people will stand up for each other... [T]he friend expects no reward for his feelings. He does not wish the performance of any duty in return, he does not view the person he has chosen as a friend with any illusion, he sees his faults and accepts him with all their consequences. Such is the ideal.
>
> (Marai 1942, pp. 126–8)

Indeed, it is – for without realizing it, Marai here is not actually writing about *philia*, but rather *agape*, which is the purest and most refined kind of love.

Agape draws on, but goes beyond, aspects of both *eros* and *philia*, identifying a perfect kind of love that is at once both a charity and a passion. It is a theological, specifically Christian, rendering of love, according to which a person's love of God is realized in his love for God's creation – chiefly for other people, and without distinction or discrimination between them. As Jesus is reported to have said: 'If you love only those who love you, what reward can you expect? ... There must be no limit to your Goodness ...' (Matthew's Gospel, 5, 46–48). As such, *agape* possesses the features of unselfishness, equality, creativity and stability which enable those who seek to aspire to it to break through the barrier of selection which features so much as a limiting characteristic of both *eros* and *philia*. Put another way, *agape* makes *eros* responsible, while elevating at the same time the preferential love of *philia* into universal love. The Christian theologian Paul Tillich translates this outcome in terms that affirm its unconditional nature 'which accepts the Other, in spite of resistance. It suffers and forgives. It seeks the personal fulfilment of the Other' (1953, p. 311).

The ethically superior nature of *agape* places this model of love at the very pinnacle of a life lived ethically. Indeed, as Armstrong says, it instructs us that being human is fundamentally a matter of growing in love – 'it is *the* meaning and purpose of each individual existence. Nothing matters as much' (2003, p. 119). Marai concurs, putting into Henrik's mouth the notion that 'without such an ideal, there would be no point to life'. St Paul, of course, said all of this much earlier on, in his letter to the wayward congregation at Corinth: 'Love is always patient and kind; love is not jealous or boastful; it is not arrogant or rude (1 Cor. 13.4)'; 'Make love your aim' (1 Cor. 14.1). We do not know how Paul's injunction was received at the time, but it is not difficult to hazard a guess, for it is, at a practical level, difficult to live at such a high pitch of unselfishness for very long, if at all. For *agape*, however interpreted, requires a degree of loving fellow-feeling that seems to transcend all earthly cares and obstacles.

Love's unifying quality

Aspects of each of *eros*, *philia* and *agape* find issue in the concept of love promoted by Romanticism. Wordsworth, for example, proclaims in *The Prelude* that love is the alpha and omega of his poetry and the source of all value in life, though his favoured models of it in practice are its maternal and marital manifestations, which might seem a slightly limited vision of love's reach, if only for the fact that each is conceived by him in terms which bring to mind the special calling of *agape*. Shelley, on the other hand, and in major contrast, makes *eros* his ideal of love, emphasizing its sexual aspects, in particular the erotic attraction felt by men and women for one another. Different again is Coleridge's paradigm of love which, like Marai's Henrik's, is friendship. This may seem bizarre, given Coleridge's ruptured relationships with Wordsworth and other people (see Holmes 1999b, p. 99n for the extent of this). Excusing such discrepancies, we learn that Coleridge, at least at the level of theory, conceives of loving friendship in a way that associates it strongly with esteem. He says precisely this in a letter to Humphrey Davy, written and sent in the second half of 1821: 'But you know that I honour you, and that I love whom I honour. *Love and Esteem with me have no dividual Being*' (my emphasis).

Coleridge's theoretical ideal of love, however, has a grandeur that is much more than the high esteem genuine friends feel for each other. Such acts of reverence, he insists, must be reflections of a bigger, specifically transcendental, scheme of things. As Singer observes, Coleridge believed strongly, and ultimately, in the metaphysical nature and power of love, in particular its 'craving for unity, for a oneness that eliminates all sense of separation between man and his environment, between one person and another, and within each individual' (Singer 1984, p. 288). Coleridge himself explains the matter thus: 'Love is a desire of the whole being to be united to some thing, or some being, felt necessary by its completeness, by the most perfect means that nature allows, and reason permits' ('Lectures on Shakespeare' [*Romeo and Juliet*]). Love, thus conceived, constitutes a kind of 'merging' (Scruton 1986, pp. 229–33 and 214–44), in the course of which the lover 'comes more and more to sympathize with the beloved, to identify with him; less and less to distinguish his desires, projects, conceptions and beliefs from her own' (Fisher 1990, p. 26). The responsibilities of such love flow easily from it: to be open; to be sensitive; to be sincere; to be concerned; to be connected; to be empathic; to be tolerant; to be respectful – virtues which I will later on associate strongly with a form of good teaching conceived as loving pedagogy. In loving others in such ways we help to complete ourselves, quite apart from other people, a view that finds explicit expression in this remarkable passage taken from another of Coleridge's letters written in 1822 and sent to Thomas Allsop:

> I love but few – but those I love I love as my soul – for I feel without them I should – not indeed cease to be kind and effluent; but – by little and little become a soul-less fixed Star, receiving no rays nor influences into my Being, a solitude, which I so tremble at that I cannot attribute it even to Divine Nature.

The people whom Coleridge loves, he loves 'as his soul', as the missing parts of himself for which he searches. Only in loving them, he tells us, can he be in any sense a whole self; and only by receiving his love are other people able to complete themselves. Love is good to the beloved because it is an inherently pleasurable affirmation of their value. But equally it is good to the lover since to love someone is necessarily to experience the beloved as good *for oneself*. As Badhwar (2005) reminds us, this insight has its origins in Aristotle's observation that 'love is like production', which is meant to draw attention to the degree to which loving is positively consequential for the self-actualization of all concerned, enabling *both* the lover and the beloved to live more vivid and enjoyable lives. Important in this equation is also the seemingly odd idea that loving requires lovers to love themselves. This idea is not designed to elevate to the level of moral principle any form of personal arrogance or vanity, but rather to draw attention to the psychological fact that someone who does not like himself very much, or indeed at all, may find it difficult to sustain loving relationships with other people.

Developing this idea, Badhwar emphasizes love's generous, trusting, creative and hopeful aspects:

> To love is not only to respond to value, but also to seek value, and to expect it. This optimistic, value-seeking spirit makes love imaginative and discerning, thereby enabling the lover to perceive potential that even the beloved cannot see ... [and] *to 'take a bet' on [its] actualization, [acting] in the expectation [of bringing it about]*. The value that emerges, then, is a joint creation of the lover and beloved [*in the course of which each helps to create the identity of the other*].
>
> (Badhwar 2005, p. 53, my emphasis and changes)

Singer says much the same, drawing attention to the way in which love bestows value on the beloved, and vice versa (1966, pp. 3–23). Steiner agrees, arguing that good teaching entails a dialectical aspect: 'The "master" learns from the "disciple" and is modified by this interrelation in what becomes ... a process of exchange. Donation becomes reciprocal, as in the labyrinths of love' (2003, p. 6). Indeed, love's largesse, manifest in its capacity to perceive potential in the beloved which he or she is either ignorant of or in denial about, articulating with a loving optimism to find ways of drawing it out, are arguably the hallmarks of effective teaching conceived as loving pedagogy.

Love's capacity to fill out the missing parts both of oneself and others, so as to make each more whole, however, is not ultimately limited in Coleridge's treatment by the power of reason. On the contrary, where love is concerned, feelings matter far more than cognition. To that extent, Coleridge was influenced as much by the empiricism of David Hume as by any Platonic conception of love. Hume had argued in the middle of the eighteenth century that reason is always the slave of the passions, which meant for him that our experience of the world depends in the final analysis upon a kind of animal faith that derives from our feelings rather than from our minds. It is not that Coleridge and his fellow Romantics, believed that 'feeling is all', but rather that feeling for them is primary – in morals, in the acquisition of knowledge about the world and in the proper pursuit of love. By implication, I will want ultimately to argue in this chapter, it is also primary in those ways of teaching that promote effective learning.

Love's contemporary elusiveness

Before I develop and reach that conclusion, I need to acknowledge a basic problem. For while we might agree with Coleridge that loving feelings rather than calculation should always be to the fore in our dealings with each other, there is, in our own time, and in late modern societies especially, the dilemma of how adequately to sustain intimate caring relationships in contexts where fixed and durable bonds are increasingly difficult to maintain. Put another way, while, today, we seem able easily to 'fall in love', and even to 'be in love', the problem we face is how to 'stay in love'. Linked to this is a modern illusion in which we are encouraged to think of relationships as perfectible and, when they prove not to be, disposable.

This sobering observation finds expression in the writings of a number of contemporary and influential social theorists. Anthony Giddens' diagnoses of the personal sphere in late modern societies, for example, draws attention to the emergence of 'pure' or 'convenience relationships', which are 'sought only for what [they] ... can bring to the partners involved', and which are closely aligned to a form of sexuality that is not tied, as hitherto, to the needs of reproduction (1992, pp. 2 and 27). This type of relationship involves a new version of love, which Giddens calls 'confluent love' – a form of love that assumes an active opening up on the part of one partner towards the other which undermines, replaces even, the patriarchy and gender imbalances characteristic of traditional, premodern, notions of intimacy.

This 'opening up', however, carries with it enormous hazards, since nowadays in particular there is no telling how things will pan out as a result. Zygmunt Bauman has written about this better than most. In his wonderfully titled study *Liquid Love: On the Frailty of Human Bonds* (2003) he draws attention to love's fluidity and brevity at the current juncture, and the degree to which entering intimate relationships today is fraught with huge risks, as 'all creation is [now] never sure where it is going to end' (p. 6), chiefly because it no longer has the acknowledged secure roots of past times. We now live highly precarious and loosely coupled intimate existences, experienced under and constituted by conditions of endemic uncertainty and transience. Moreover, freed from the anchors of tradition, which used to help us to form secure expectations, people are compelled now to make things up as they go along, including how best to construct and conduct their loving selves: 'love is a mortgage loan drawn on an uncertain, and inscrutable, future' (2003, p. 8). Beck and Beck-Gernsheim's earlier overlapping analysis of intimacy in the modern age, *The Normal Chaos of Love*, reaches the same conclusion as Bauman:

> it is now no longer possible to pronounce in some binding way what family, marriage, parenthood, sexuality or love mean, what they should or could be; rather, these vary in substance, exceptions, norms and morality, from individual to individual and from relationship to relationship. The answers to the above must be worked out, negotiated, arranged and justified in all the details of how, what, why or why not ... *Love* [has become] ... *a blank that the lovers must fill in themselves, across the widening trenches of biography.*
>
> (Beck and Beck-Gernsheim, 1995, p. 5, my emphasis)

Possessing no permanent attachments, the members of late modern society must therefore tie whatever bonds they can to engage with one another using their own wits, skill *and* dedication – an undertaking requiring considerable maturity of reason *and* feeling. To that extent, love is now, *more than ever before*, an achievement, a 'truth' brilliantly enunciated by Armstrong:

> it is something we create, individually, not something we just find, if only we are lucky enough. [And] ... it is not something which can be forced simply by effort. You can't just sit down and decide to love someone ... This is unsurprising if we reflect that love is dependent upon many other achievements: kindness of interpretation, sympathy, understanding ... And these kinds of capacity and awareness do not spring suddenly into being. Each requires patient *cultivation* ... [And] if this is true of loving, it is also true of being lovable. Being lovable cannot ... be separated from being a good person in general ...
>
> (Armstrong 2003, p. 158)

A loving pedagogy

So, where do Romantic conceptions of love, and analyses of its contemporary elusiveness, leave the prospects and the tasks of school education? Certainly each suggests some rethinking of its overall purposes, for if loving, after Coleridge, helps to make us whole – contributing to the creation not only of one's own identity, but also of the identities of others – then its cultivation surely must be a significant aim for education, including an underpinning principle of effective pedagogy. And, certainly, too, if love is a particularly demanding achievement at the moment, then education needs to consider how best to assist pupils to acquire the competences necessary for bringing it about and holding on to and nurturing it in their lives. Moreover, if children, as is increasingly understood, learn about styles of relating, including those entailed in love itself, through seeing and experiencing how adults relate significantly to them and to one another, then the conclusion must be drawn that teachers have a special responsibility to develop forms of pedagogy that give high priority to love's most salient features. These, we learned earlier, when discussing aspects of *philia*, include being: open, sensitive, sincere, concerned, connected, empathic, tolerant, respectful, to which, given what I said a moment ago, can be added kind in one's interpretations and sympathetic in one's understanding of others.

These qualities exemplify not only the love that teachers should have for their pupils, which provides the best possible basis for teaching them well, but also the goodness they must embody in how they conduct themselves at work in order to be respected and loved by them in return, thus facilitating in the classroom and elsewhere in school the sort of loving merger to which I made reference earlier. Teachers need to be good people in their own right, and the moral basis of this, as I stressed at the beginning of this book, is a fundamental and deep respect for pupils as *persons*. Central to such respect is a loving faith in what they can achieve, amounting often to much more than what they think, a conclusion which also recalls to mind what I have said about the optimistic value-seeking nature of love generally.

Central also is for teachers to have sufficient confidence that they can make a worthwhile difference in the classroom, possessing the skills and enthusiasm to bring this about. Good teachers, on this understanding, must love not just what they teach but, additionally, their ability to foster effective learning among their pupils through teaching them well. In other words, to pick up again on another prior point, which stated that loving requires lovers to love themselves, an effective teacher is someone who is in love with their facility to teach; and, where relevant ability is lacking, the good teacher, like the good lover, finds a way to fill in the missing elements, growing in pedagogical love as a result through being concerned to take better care of the beloved – the child as learning subject.

Loving pedagogy is thus about being willing to move beyond oneself as a teacher in order to cultivate pupils in all manner of important ways, including emotionally, intellectually and spiritually. When teachers love their pupils in this fashion, their generosity is likely to be reciprocated, resulting in them being nurtured in similar kinds of ways in return.

Indeed, it is chiefly through a pedagogic love of this kind, entailing a striving for the evolution of somebody else, that teachers and pupils, *together*, are able better to grow and mature. Garrison makes this same point:

> in creating the conditions necessary for a child to learn and grow, teachers are bestowing value (that is, a Good) on the child. In creating value, teachers [also] find self-expression, learning and personal growth. By learning to recognize and respond appropriately to the needs, desires, and interests of each unique child in their class, teachers have their own needs, desires, and interests fulfilled as well.
>
> (Garrison 1997, p. 40)

To interpret such loving learning relationships between teachers and pupils as a form of overfamiliar encroachment is then completely to misunderstand their nature. There may be occasions when it is reasonable to invoke D.H. Lawrence's 'holy ground' principle, particularly if a teacher befriends a pupil for selfish rather than educational reasons. But no condemnation of this sort can justifiably be made, for example, of either William Taylor or Thomas Bowman, each of whose tutoring of Wordsworth at Hawkshead Grammar School, which I described in the previous chapter, was often unceremonious and sometimes very close, and thus open to being misconstrued. I trust it was made clear that neither of these teachers ever presumed to enter into relations with pupils that were disrespectful of their young age or of their relative powerlessness. They did not 'take advantage' of their pupils in general, or Wordsworth in particular; but rather sought, in appropriate intimate ways, informed by *agape*, to 'give each advantage', which is the crucial difference here. And they did so by taking extra trouble, without thought of reciprocation, though no doubt it was forthcoming, to enthuse pupils with a love of learning, which in Wordsworth's case was associated strongly with poetic self-expression and reading widely.

A similar pedagogic attitude, it will also be recalled, informed John Corrie's manner of teaching the young Hazlitt at Hackney College. In each case, these tutors exemplified pedagogic love for their pupils of an admirable kind: they befriended their pupils to benefit them educationally, and never to fuel and meet their personal needs, other than to achieve the feeling that they had done the best possible job *as teachers*. And *eros* makes an appearance too here, since Taylor, Bowman and Corrie may be evaluated as pedagogues who strove to realize the good through the manner in which they sought to bring out the best – the beautiful – in their pupils. The friendships they forged with them were based, then, on a mutual concern for the good things in life – the pursuit of knowledge and poetic sensibility, no less – which they sought to enjoy *together*. Although sexual passion was never an aspect of any of this, passionate friendship was, to the degree that each party to the relationships possessed (after Nietzsche) 'a shared higher *thirst* for an ideal above them', leading to what Mark Vernon elegantly describes in his perceptive and wise book *The Philosophy of Friendship* (2005) as a form of 'mutual separateness' that gave teacher and taught 'the gift of being able to return to their lives with a sense of new possibility' (p. 48).

Another theme from a previous chapter – that of childhood – is also relevant to what I am seeking to say here. In Chapter 2 I argued that the Romantics offer us an image of the child as the personification of hope, implying that the proper education of children represents one way of realizing optimism throughout society. The trouble is that nowadays the soul of the child is increasingly under siege, by which I mean that the momentousness of childhood is now radically being corrupted by targeted marketing which seeks to construct children as consumers rather than people (see Williams 2006). Or, to quote Bauman: 'Spirituality may be a child's birth gift, but it [is being] confiscated by the consumer markets and then redeployed to lubricate the wheels of the consumer economy' (2005, p. 115).

Campbell (1989) argues that many of the hedonistic features of modern patterns of consumption to which Bauman draws critical attention – notably fashion and an addiction to novelty generally – have their roots in Romanticism, in particular its philosophy of recreation. There is some truth in this line of reasoning, as Campbell illustrates. On the other hand, his examples do not ultimately provide sufficient support for his thesis, which seems overstated, for it cannot unequivocally be the case that Romanticism 'provided ethical support for that restless and continuous pattern of consumption which so distinguishes the behaviour of man' (Campbell 1989, p. 201). Aspects of it may have contributed to the creation of such a structure of feeling, but it is surely neither fully nor even partially to blame for its existence. The real culprit here is not a literary movement, but an economic one – nineteenth- and twentieth-century capitalism. Romanticism cannot be blamed either for the growing tendency for children today to relate to each other, and for adults to relate to children, in commodified ways, rather than through the means of intimate interpersonal relationships.

Nor can Romanticism be held to account for the gross targeting of marketing on children themselves, which provokes between them hostile jealousies, leading sometimes to horrendous bullying, grounded in absurd justifications about how someone looks, designated by the absence of particular corporate brand names on clothes and by what they do and do not own generally. Nor, again, is Romanticism to blame for the psychologically damaging effects of this process which realizes a peculiar form of insecurity in which some children worry piteously about being materially 'left behind' by their immediate peers who seem to them to possess more than they do and to look 'cool' in ways that they do not. Complementary tendencies are working their way through the process of schooling, which is routinely conceived now as being about realizing an educational 'product', whose claim to distinctiveness is the number of attainment targets children reach and the aggregate of qualifications they have acquired.

Surely in order to be complete and wholesome, childhood, and children's school learning, requires something altogether different – something which encourages the sort of hope upon which I placed so much emphasis in earlier discussion. And this is where the pedagogy of love comes to the rescue, offering a mode of relating and engagement that is grounded in the pursuit of the Good and the beautiful, both of which, unlike fashion and commercial commodities generally, are enduring and capable of fending off the excesses of our individualistic culture. As such, because loving aspires towards oneness, a pedagogy of love represents an effort, mediated through teachers' classroom practice, to reunite what late modern society increasingly separates in its headlong promotion of personal gain, providing a means of creating a new moral economy to replace the dreadful materialistic one that permeates so much feeling and thinking today.

Additionally, it anticipates educational contexts for both teachers and pupils that fully stretch imaginations and encourage more humane and joyous ways of interrelating. Maxine Greene puts it thus:

All we can do is to speak with others as passionately and eloquently as we can; all we can do is to look into each other's eyes and urge each other on to new beginnings. Our classrooms ought to be nurturing and thoughtful and just, all at once; they ought to pulsate with multiple conceptions of what it is to be human and alive. They ought to resound with the voices of articulate young people in dialogues always incomplete because there is always more to be discovered and more to be said. We must want our students to achieve friendship as each one stirs to wide-awakeness, to imaginative action, and to renewed consciousness of possibility.

(Greene 1995, in Goldstein 2004, p. 46)

Teaching through such loving relations of course demands a classroom dynamic that is intimate and earnest, bordering on the passionate, the nature of which I will try to describe in the final section of this chapter.

Lessons from the Romantics about passion

Reintroducing the Romantic concept of love into public discourse about education is, then, imperative, not least because far too many of the most salient features of current educational practice in schools entail modes of negative technocratic hyper-rationality. These require pupils and their teachers to relate at a distance from one another through the medium of official goals and associated modes of formal assessment. As Liston and Garrison entreat teachers, and by implication their pupils, are made, educationally, for better, more Romantic, things: 'Teachers have loving, caring and connecting reasons for doing things mere instrumental rationality will never know' (2004, p. 10). The so-called 'virtues' of teaching underscore this point. Hogan draws up a list of them which interestingly reflects those in Coleridge's model of friendship: 'circumspect honesty, patience and persistence, frankness, originality, a judicious faith in pupils ... and a *categorical sense of care* for them' (1996, p. 16, my emphasis). In creating this list, Hogan daringly reaffirms a moral and ultimately Romantic role for the teacher as a significant and influential adult figure dedicated to the business of loving her pupils in 'structures of pedagogic relation' infused with 'reciprocal trust' (Steiner 2003, pp. 2–3) – what the Jewish theologian Martin Buber beautifully describes as a form of 'detached tenderness', in which 'the glance of the educator accepts and receives them all' (1947, p. 94).

Drawing on Iris Murdoch's (1970) Platonic interpretation of the Good, Liston takes this kind of imperative on to an exalted and ultimately explicitly Romantic level by exhorting teachers who have lost it to 'recapture that love of teaching ... which enables its exponents to venture once more into the space where hope and possibility exist' (2000, p. 94). Like Hogan, Liston argues for a re-moralizing of teaching that 'places an understanding of the good and an orientation to love at its very centre' (ibid.). This call to a larger love in pedagogy constitutes an appeal to teachers by Liston to recover 'the idea of the Good' as a focal point of professional reflection:

> [a] larger teaching love ... attends fully to the situation, to the students in their classes, in an attempt to see things more clearly, *to find ways to*

connect students with the grace of things. It looks for the Good in students and those teaching settings [they work in]; it attempts to see students in ways that assume and build up the Good.

(Liston 2000, p. 97, my emphasis)

It also requires teachers to share with and initiate their pupils into the love they have for the truth that resides in the subjects or topics they teach, which, if contemplated sufficiently, is capable of *'nourishing their souls'* (Elliott 1974, p. 147, my emphasis). This is as close to a classical Romantic sense of the sublime that one can get, I would suggest, to the degree that it conceives of effective teaching and learning as crucially about making profound connections within a sea of limitless variety – that is to say, articulations that work between the pupil's experience and the subject matter of the curriculum; and between their sense-making capacity of pupils and the enabling abilities of teachers; and, ultimately, between the limited human faculties of the understanding and the infinity of the physical universe.

This is no easy thing to achieve, of course. For loving of this kind, in pedagogy, as elsewhere, following an awe-like initial response, requires commitment, intimacy and passion, each immediately recognizable not just as defining qualities of Romanticism, but as dispositions difficult to sustain at a pitch for any length of time. Passion, even so, is *the* special quality here, providing the energy for the other two, while directing teachers simultaneously to reflect on how they should go about earnestly engaging with their pupils and the specialist fields of knowledge into which they seek to initiate them, so as to increase their commitment to and motivation for learning. As Fried enthusiastically puts it, a teacher

needs to be passionate about [his or her] field of knowledge: in love with the poetry of Emily Dickinson or the prose of Marcus Garvey; dazzled by the spiral of DNA or the swirl of Van Gogh's cypresses; intrigued by the origins of the Milky Way or the demise of the Soviet Empire; delighted by the sound of Mozart or the sonority of French vowels; a maniac for health and fitness or wild about algebraic word problems.

(Fried 1995, p. 18)

As such, passionate teachers need to express themselves to the full, even when their efforts receive little or nothing in return.

Another way of thinking about this is to invoke the word 'gusto', the critical term that lies behind and prompts Hazlitt's creative project. Throughout Hazlitt's oeuvre, but particularly in his short essay 'On

Gusto', this word points up an essential exuberance of expression and invention – 'intensely realized and widely diffused, possessing sensuous vividness' (Bromwich 1999, p. 229) – as found in the work of particular painters and writers he especially admires and commends, including, as in the following extract, Titian, Shakespeare and Milton:

> Gusto in art is power or passion defining any object . . . There is gusto in the colouring of Titian. Not only do his heads seem to think – his bodies seem to feel . . . As the objects themselves in nature would produce an impression on the sense, distinct from every other object, and having something divine in it, which the heart owns and the imagination consecrates, the objects in the picture preserve the same impression, absolute, unimpaired, stamped with all the truth of passion, the pride of the eye, and the charm of beauty . . . The infinite quantity of dramatic invention in Shakespeare takes from his gusto. The power he delights to shew is not intense, but discursive . . . Milton [also] has great gusto. He repeats his blow twice; *grapples with and exhausts his subject* . . .
>
> (Wu 1998, Vol. 2, p. 79, my emphasis)

Gusto, then, is not just a property of certain art objects: it is also crucially a feature of the performance of the truly creative artist. Uncharacteristic self-effacement prevented Hazlitt from including here his own name as someone possessing gusto. For possess it he did, and in a superabundant quantity. Tom Paulin, sympathetically describing Hazlitt's literary style, refers to it as being endowed with 'sheer concentrated zing' (1998, p. 235). His critical method too was highly experiential and pragmatic, as well as informed always by a love for its subject, attributes which throughout this chapter I have sought to connect with a conception of effective loving pedagogy. Thus, in the manner in which Hazlitt carried an energy in him as he went about his creative work, I want to insist that a pedagogy of love needs similarly to be undertaken with sparkle, brio and zip, including, on occasion, a feverish emotional engagement.

Here is how Hazlitt translates this imperative into the business of writing poetry: 'The principle of writing poetry is a very anti-levelling principle. It aims at effect, it exists by contrast. It admits no medium. It does everything by excess. It rises above the ordinary standard of sufferings and crimes. *It presents a dazzling experience*' (Wu 1998, Vol. 1, p. 126, my emphasis). This is from Hazlitt's discussion of *Coriolanus* in his *Characters of Shakespeare's Plays*. While characteristically overstated, it communicates an important insight – that *some meanings only get started through immoderateness*, which of course is so resonate with the first feelings of love. For sure, things must eventually calm down, both in life and in the classroom, but exuberance in both has an important place, providing a sense of potential: 'a sense of something evermore about to be' (Bloom 1986, p. 4).

While all of what Hazlitt here, and Fried earlier, says is true, it needs to be tempered by warnings that passion and gusto in the classroom, if left unchecked and undiluted, are as likely to underplay, overwhelm, exclude even, the interests and experiences of pupils, as to meet properly and engage fully with their educational needs. As Comte-Sponville cautions, 'passion has something monomaniacal about it' (2003, p. 258). Accordingly, care needs to be taken in how it is used in developing a theoretical pedagogy of love. Indeed, Fried anticipates this concern, arguing that

> passionate teachers organize and focus their passionate interests by getting to the heart of their subject matter and *sharing with their students* some of what lies there ... They convey their passion ... by *acting as partners in learning*, rather than as experts in the field. As partners, they *invite* [them] to search for knowledge and insightful experiences, and they build confidence and competence among students who might otherwise choose to sit back and watch their teacher do and say interesting things.
>
> (Fried 1995, p. 6, my emphasis)

These sentiments are an antidote to the pressures exerted by some teachers who, being so full of their own knowledge and a fervent wish to 'pass it on', neglect and override the experience the children bring with them into school.

To be a passionate teacher is not the same then as being a charismatic one – that is to say, the sort of teacher who, in Alex Moore's words, promotes his or her own personality, possessing an 'inherent popularity, and intangible ability to enthuse and inspire students' (2004, p. 55). Of course such teachers are capable of doing a good job, but their numbers are few, and they can sometimes impede the educational progress of pupils and colleagues who prefer to learn and teach in less dramatic and self-gratifying ways. No, the sort of passion being argued for here is the kind that places the greatest emphasis not on charisma, but on a form of earnestness about teaching, which Chris Day associates with

> enthusiasm, caring commitment and hope ...; with fairness and understanding ...; with being close rather than distant; with having a

good sense of playfulness; with encouraging students to learn in different ways; with relating learning to experience; with encouraging students to take responsibility for their own learning ...; [and] with being knowledgeable about their subject; with creating learning environments that engage students and stimulate in them an excitement to learn.

(Day 2004, pp. 12–13)

Such teachers have 'a genuine concern for the Truth which they know is "a passionate business"' (Peters 1973, p. 101). They have also a commitment to the Good, which they mediate through their love of what they teach and the love they have for their pupils. Through this process, pupils are helped to see the true value of what they are invited to study, which is regarded by them as precious by virtue of the teacher's love for it. Although they are not simply defined teacher-heroes, such educators act with heroic passion to encourage pupil learning, an observatino that anticipates the subject of the next chapter which explores the role of heroism in promoting effective pedagogy and better school management.

5

Heroizing Pedagogy and School Management

It is impossible to teach without the courage to try a thousand times before giving up.

(*Paulo Freire*)

The last great age of heroes?

Heroism is a significant leitmotif of Romantic discernment. It is also, I will argue in this chapter, a potent, yet often overlooked, condition for teaching and learning effectively and leading successfully in schools. This is not a fashionable view in education, I admit – indeed it is one that many working in the field baulk at instinctively, fearing that it gives undue prominence to certain individuals (usually identified as brash, conceited and self-assured men). Its conventional association with high-flown and valiant conduct merely adds to the critical mix, especially today when so much of educational culture emphasizes the virtues of 'inclusion', downplaying the 'special' and 'distinctive'.

Talk about heroes, in education and generally, also evokes negative images of hero-worship, including portraits of naïve people being easily beguiled by the special charisma of extraordinary personalities who use their powers of influence to subjugate and exploit. These are understandable concerns, about which history teaches us to be alert. But they are surely not the whole story. Inasmuch as there are positive conceptions of the heroic from which education might benefit and upon which some of its practice might be modelled.

The 'Big Six' Romantic poets certainly did not shy away from heroism, often representing to themselves and their readers the importance of daring to struggle heroically for some form of inner authenticity as the basis for personal imaginative freedom and growth. Writing poetry, for Wordsworth, was *the* means to this end, for it created within him a mood in which he enjoyed feelings greater than he ordinarily knew. All the other Romantic poets discussed in this book felt and said much the same. So, while most of them viewed humanity as essentially flawed, partaking in original sin no less, they believed also that it possessed a remarkable potential capable of heroic redemption, providing imaginative effort is exerted. In seeking to follow such a life, each poet had a character of great vitality through which he sought to express his free spirit, frequently in large, long poems of epic proportions and implications. Hazlitt was much the same, though on a much smaller scale, using prose writing rather than poetry to make his point.

Because the Romantic period was one of rebellion – social, political, moral and philosophical – it quickly became an age of heroes. Indeed, the 'Big Six' poets, and Hazlitt to a lesser extent, satisfied a particular taste of an era, giving to it in their writings a surfeit of heroes – all passion and fiery energy, all moral, intellectual and political disaffection. The rebellious individualism of the characters they wrote about, not to mention their own personalities, articulates fully with certain key aspects of the times in which they lived. So, while every historical period has its rebels and heroes, the Romantic one had arguably more than its fair share, chiefly because the contemporary changes in English social life and thought were crucial and fundamental, requiring a heroic response of one kind or another.

Richardson (1994) suggests that a 'dual revolution' was underway in England in the second half of the eighteenth century – sociopolitical, in the first instance, and industrial–commercial, in the second. The loss of the American colonies and defeat by France in 1783 represented a massive shock to English national pride. Political issues in England simultaneously became more turbulent than they had been for 50 years, with the assertion of radicalism evident in some parts of its culture, and the defence of conservatism manifest in others. Hazlitt, in particular, chiefly though his journalism, was significantly involved in these debates, combating the forces of reaction, as he saw them, with fierce polemics. But his was not a lone voice. There were many intellectuals in late-eighteenth-century England who had been influenced by US and continental revolutionary and socialist ideas. These inspired them to challenge and demand changes in existing political institutions, not least to ameliorate the miseries felt by many people experiencing the dreadful consequences of increased unplanned urbanization, trade dislocation and periodic famine.

Outcasts, outsiders and solitaries

The origins of the kind of discontent with which Hazlitt and the 'Big Six' poets became associated are not difficult to identify. Nor is it surprising that the country's governing class at the time reacted in turn by unleashing a maelstrom of fear and misgiving about the radicalism they represented and encouraged – an effort on its part which may partially account for the degree to which many of the Romantics acted out in their own lives the parallel heroic roles of 'outcast' and 'outsider'. In Wordsworth's and Coleridge's cases, this led them to set themselves apart from the rest of society by withdrawing to the Cumbrian countryside. There was also an element of snobbishness in all of this, reflected in the view, certainly found in Wordsworth's outlook, that a poet was someone possessed 'of more than usual organic sensibility', having a 'greater knowledge of human nature, and a more comprehensive soul' than the common man (see the Preface to the *Lyrical Ballads*).

While such arrogant elitism does not flatter the Romantic poets, it does help to explain why the heroic characters that appear in their writings are often alienated and isolated. The heroes of the 'Big Six', for example, are nearly always, like themselves, solitaries – Northumberland dalesmen or disillusioned hermits (Wordsworth and Keats); intellectual rebels like Faust (Shelley and Byron); moral outcasts or wanderers like Cain (Coleridge and Byron) and Ahasuerus (Coleridge, Byron and Shelley); or rebels against society and even against God, like Prometheus (Byron and Shelley) and Lucifer (Byron).

Heroism and revolution

Such hero-types bear with them aspects of the mood of the age when they first appeared, especially its political and social ethos, one aspect of which, as mentioned a moment ago, included the fear and promise of radical change, which is why all of the Romantic poets sought to communicate the significance for English life of the massive upheavals underway in revolutionary France from 1789. Indeed, just as the French Revolution was considered to be the physical realization of the Enlightenment, so the poetry of the British Romantics, notably the *Lyrical Ballads* of Worsdworth and Coleridge, was conceived by its producers as a form of revolution carried out at the level of words. As Duff argues,'Romanticism sought to effect in poetry what revolution aspired to achieve in politics: innovation, transformation, de-familiarisation' (1998, p. 26).

The personality and career of Napoleon Bonaparte was central to this process. While Napoleon is an ambiguous figure in any discussion of Romanticism, most of the Romantics admired enormously, certainly initially, his genius and Promethean-like achievements, which they glorified and commended. Although history tells us that Napoleon's libertarianism gave way quickly to authoritarian militarism, as a middle-class self-made man he embodied the spirit of the Revolution, instituting, as he did, far-reaching social and legal reforms. As the educational philosopher Kieran Egan observes, Napoleon, *at that time*, and at the height of his powers, significantly 'transformed people's consciousness of what was politically possible. He embodied, in awe-inspiring degree, force of will, energy, ingenuity, power, and an absolute recklessness about long-standing political, social and legal conventions' (1990, pp. 23 and 30).

No wonder, then, that many of the Romantic poets found Napoleon inspirational; and no wonder, too, that his potent symbolic and mythic status exerted such a profound influence on their thinking and writing. He seemed to personify, to an extraordinary extent, many of the qualities they associated with the heroic – compassion, courage, tenacity, tolerance, wit, ingenuity and patience. These were things they valued and sought to replicate in their own lives and to commend to their readers.

The inner hero

While Napoleon's heroism exerted an astonishing poetic sway on most of the 'Big Six', I am not suggesting that Napoleon should influence directly the way we think about educational practice. However, I think it is a feasible idea that teachers might want to look for ways to assist their pupils to draw on the possibilities of heroism. While this is significantly to do with helping pupils to avoid having low expectations of themselves, it is also about identifying approaches to learning that bring them into close empathetic contact with subject matter which vividly depicts high achievement and with which they can easily and sympathetically identify – subject matter that helps them, so to speak, 'to "try-on" for a while certain transcendent qualities which they are likely to admire or wonder at' (Egan 1992, p. 82). The philosopher Richard Rorty suggests something similar in his invitation to liberal educators to consider ways in which they can better assist their students to heroicize those people who 'dissolve the problems of their day by transcending the vocabulary in which these problems [are commonly] posed' (1982, p. 10). Significantly, and in the light of what has already been said about love and pedagogy, Rorty defines his version of liberal education teaching in explicitly Romantic terms: 'General studies is a catchword for the sort of education which aims at Romance ... Teaching [them] is erotic or nothing' (pp. 10 and 13).

Egan has, more than anyone else, pioneered this approach. His advocacy of it is based upon a simple enough premise – that, by getting close to and *internalizing* aspects of the lives of particular heroic figures, people can sometimes help themselves to overcome difficulties which might otherwise seem overwhelming. Egan makes this point elegantly and persuasively, arguing that 'by associating with whomever in the world seems best to transcend [the threats posed by external reality and personal circumstances], we too feel some security against them as well, some confidence that we might transcend them also' (1991, p. 90). Indeed, such associations appear to satisfy a subconscious need we all have for someone to admire – a model tucked away in our imagination, so to speak, for encouragement. Reciting Bertolt Brecht's famous dramatic aphorism that it is an unhappy land that looks for heroes (*The Life of Galileo*) does not alter this fact. A land without heroes may indeed be all the better for not having them, particularly when they take the form of megalomaniacal dictators (the threat of which is a central theme of Brecht's play). But, as Hughes-Hallett has recently stated, 'only a fortunate land is confident enough to dispense [altogether] with heroes' (2004, p. 2), and ours is arguably not one of them, even if we might wish it to be. Accordingly, while I retain, and would always encourage in others, a natural wariness of the potentially pernicious effects of uncritical forms of hero-worship, I am not immune to the inspirational nature of particular heroes. There is nothing wrong or inadequate in this, leading me to argue that the issue is not about the need to abandon in pedagogy the significance of the hero, but to reflect carefully on which heroes, educationally speaking, are most worthy of mention in the curriculum.

Egan is always careful to discourage teachers from inviting pupils to associate with archetypical male heroes, particularly ones that only know how to achieve their objectives through force. On the contrary, he argues that this approach works only if pupils are able to find their own heroes. What matters, he insists, is that such exemplars help to create an increased knowledge and awareness of those heroic qualities that overcome the things which for much of the time constrain us. For the hero is the man or woman who has been able to battle through his or her personal limitations to arrive at a state in which what ordinarily holds them back is put aside. This, then, is not a case of endorsing the histrionic lifestyles of today's celebrity heroes, who are largely media-manufactured. Rather, it is matter of taking seriously those aims of education that stress its role in enabling children to become confident people: a process which can be assisted through teaching and learning tasks that highlight particular individuals who exemplify heroic qualities in their lives.

There is a need to handle this idea with great care, of course. For a start, it is unlikely to benefit all pupils, some of whom might feel less confident if the behaviour of a singular hero is put before them as a universal ideal. In my case, for example, I just know I could never be like my sporting hero, the US cyclist Lance Armstrong. Indeed, sometimes just thinking about what he does on a bicycle (Armstrong 2001) makes me feel worse about myself as a cyclist. On the other hand, contemplating his sporting achievements – particularly in overcoming cancer and returning to pro-racing – also stirs me to try that bit harder on my bike, or to complain less about riding it up 8 per cent hills. But, as this autobiographical reference makes clear, being inspired by Lance is never a substitute for having a go myself, which highlights a further worry about naïve kinds of hero-worship, about which Hughes-Hallet offers this important warning: 'An exaggerated veneration for an exceptional individual poses an insidious temptation. It allows worshippers to abnegate responsibility, looking to the great man [or great woman] for salvation or for fulfilment that they should more properly be working to accomplish for themselves' (2004, p. 3). This warning is very much heeded in my approach here, since as I am *not* advocating the inculcation of hero-devotion as an educational end, but rather the use of *hero-internalization* as a resource for improving children's motivation and achievement.

Favourite heroes and heroines

Many people have favourite heroes whom they find particularly inspiring. In my case these are individuals that astonish me by their steadfastness in the face of shocking difficulty, and who give me hope that the lesser problems I face can be overcome. I mentioned the cyclist Lance Armstrong in this connection earlier on. But consider also the sailor Ellen MacArthur, who for two years battled against rough seas and swelling storms in the middle of the South Atlantic Ocean during her solo round-the-world record voyage. As if the elements weren't enough for her to have to cope with, Ellen had to withstand and overcome a series of on-board technical disasters as well first, a lack of drinking water caused by poorly functioning purifiers, and, second, a failed generator, causing toxic fumes to circulate throughout the enclosed areas of her trimaran. Together, these problems threatened to scupper her attempt on the record. She admits that at one point she nearly gave up: 'It took me hours to work out the problem with the water intake system . . . Eventually, I got it going and at least now I have a few litres of fresh drinking water . . . I got some sleep, but I need a lot more. I nearly had to pull out – it was that close. I got to the stage where I couldn't even breathe on the boat ... I was about at my wits' end ...' (Hopps 2004).

Two days later, having single-handedly band-aided each fault, Ellen is able to put a more optimistic slant on continuing: 'The difference in my outlook between now and 48 hours ago is absolutely black and white. I've had some terrible issues [to deal with], and it really did seem like the odds were stacked against me for a long period of time. The boat seems back on track now ... So, things are much better, and my outlook is much more positive' (Grice 2004).

Ellen's positive outlook on this occasion was similarly tested during the Vendee Globe round-the-world race. On Christmas Eve, 2000, nearing Cape Horn, she was forced, with winds blowing at 30 knots, to climb 200 feet of mast to replace her boat's halyard, the poor condition of which was making abandoning the race the only next possible course. She writes: 'As I took the mast in my hands and began the climb I felt almost as if I was stepping on the moon – a world over which I had no control ... Eyes closed and teeth gritted, I hung on tight, wrists clinched together, and hoped [for the best] ... I managed to make it to the top, but now I was exhausted. I squinted at the grey sky above me and watched the mast-head whip across the clouds. ... Below me, the sea stretched out for ever, the size and length of the waves emphasized by this aerial view. This [I thought] is what it must look like to the albatross' (MacArthur, 2003, pp. 292–3). Ellen restored the halyard, and slowly inched her way back down the mast to the safety of her vessel's deck. Reading her after-the-event account of this repair is dramatic enough; seeing it 'live' on the video film she made as she attempted it confirms its truth – that it was an amazingly heroic thing for her to have done.

A few days later Ellen 'rounds the Horn', emailing home as she does this diary extract:

Well, I feel quite overwhelmed ... The stress and difficulties of the last few days seem to be melting into emotion as I approach the Horn. ... I cannot help but feel moved deep inside me [thinking] of past storms and other struggles off this point.

This race has been hard; but when I think of those [sailors] here hundreds of years ago I feel very humble sitting here. For then, the corner was literally life or death, and my heart goes out to all those who have struggled, survived and died on this piece of water ... EACH TIME I think of where we are, and where we've been, I find my eyes welling with tears. It's been a long haul since the launch in NZ, and the most incredible journey of my life. Not just the story of a GIRL ALONE ON THE SEA, BUT FAR MORE THAN THAT. For me, it's a story of teamwork, friendship and love – the story of so many people working towards a goal ... I feel there are so many others with me on board; I've never been lonely – far from it – even in times of stress.

(MacArthur 2003, pp. 319–20)

Enthralling and inspiring, Ellen's achievements beggar belief. You don't have to be a sailor to find them emboldening. She simply cannot do things by half. There is no doubt either that Ellen has become the main driving force behind the British public's current enthusiasm for sailing, because it can identify with what she does and how she does it, even though most people do not sail, and are unlikely ever to do so. Of course, her courage, determination and will to win through, whatever the odds against, arise in the course of participating in a sports event which many people might judge as absurd, over-sponsored, and entirely inconsequential. That's as maybe. But individuals like Ellen MacArthur are the sort of people most likely to communicate to children the idea that not all the big difficulties they encounter, in learning specifically and in life generally, need always overwhelm, encouraging the feeling that they too might overcome.

Another personal heroine of mine is Jane Tomlinson. Terminally ill with cancer, she undertakes, with her brother, a charity tandem-cycle ride, from Rome to her home in Leeds, in order to raise £1 million to help combat her disease (Tomlinson and Tomlinson 2005). She sets out barely able to stand because of the pain in her legs: 'There's a level of pain all the time ... and sometimes it can be very distressing, but I see it as part of my life. I mean, what am I going to do: sit in a chair and be sad? There's still a life to be lived. I'd rather get on with it' (Adams 2004, p. 23). In the course of her marathon, Jane rides her bicycle through the sorts of mountain passes some of us would consider detouring around if we were in a car. How, for example, she managed to pedal up, without once pushing, the leg-shattering Mont Ventoux in the French Alps is hard to comprehend, particularly for this serious biker who has. But she did, exemplifying perfectly the sort of heroic qualities capable of impressing and inspiring anyone, and not just children in school. The fact that Jane, like Ellen, is a woman, moreover, provides added value to the account and the achievement it reports, given that heroism is all too often gendered along exclusively masculine lines.

I am hoping that the point I am trying to make here is by now clear. Simply, it is about teachers using specific examples of heroism as a means of assisting pupils to consider ways in which they might replicate heroic actions in their own lives, in however small a way, and so make more of themselves.

Teachers as heroes

Teachers, as well as pupils, can benefit from a brush with the heroic, particularly those who work in settings which frustrate and compromise their best intentions, or who lack the courage and confidence to try out new things. By engaging with and internalizing particular heroic qualities, which might include how colleagues similarly positioned to themselves are better able to cope with demands on their competence, there is the chance they might develop new hope in their own professional lives.

Arguably, too, a re-engagement with the transcendental nature of the educational process itself, which has its own heroic aspects, including the awesome power to lead us into new modes of understanding and appreciation, will make this outcome more likely. The sort of 'teacher-hero' I have in mind here is not the 'saviour-teacher' described by Alex Moore – that is, a teacher who, in seeking 'the undying love and gratitude' of her pupils, teaches 'through circumstances rather than through choice', privileging a 'highly individualized teaching style' that draws attention to her 'classroom persona as much as – perhaps more than – the substance of her lessons' (2004, pp. 57 and 65). Instead, what I am commending is a form of teaching that recognizes its heroic aspects in terms that stress the importance of teachers striving hard to identify and put into practice imaginative solutions to how better to teach and promote learning in situations where this is not always easy. It is this sort of heroism that exemplifies teaching as a what we call 'vocation'.

Such vocationalism requires courage, entailing a willingness to take risks, sometimes at a cost to oneself. While courage of course does not discriminate between honest and evil ends, it remains the virtue of heroes. It is also a necessary virtue in teaching. The courageous teacher-hero on this interpretation is someone who bravely and disinterestedly seeks to serve the needs of others; who takes moral duty and personal authenticity seriously; and who eschews cowardice in the pursuit of the common good. As Chris Day states:

it takes courage not to be discouraged when teaching practices must be changed, new curricula observed, news rules of conduct met ... Teaching well, over time, is a struggle and it takes courage to continue to encourage self and others to learn in changing personal, professional, social, and organizational contexts.

(Day 2004, p. 31)

The rebellious individualism that is so characteristic of British Romanticism of course does not fit in at all with the more collegial vision that Day commends here. Some of the Romantic poets, as we learned earlier, were literally isolated from the society of their day, engaging with it only indirectly through their work. They did not join political parties and they only infrequently and selectively aligned themselves with specific political reforms. Their heroes were much the same. Like themselves, they were rebels and outsiders, and in equal measure. The alienated Gothic Villain, Noble Outlaw and Faust-like figures that feature so much in their lists of heroic types are thus not helpful exemplars of the public-service ethic that Day is concerned to encourage among today's teachers. On the contrary, such figures are often detached and austere, and nearly always superior-minded solitaries, characteristics totally at odds not only with Day's conception of the courageous teacher but also with the passionate teacher outlined in the previous chapter.

School leaders as heroes

Nor do these austere solitaries chime in with progressive notions of school management, complementing rather the austere disdainfulness embodied in the behaviour of those sorts of headteachers (wrongly now thought extinct) who lead their institutions by a mix of bullying and domination, in the course of which junior staff can be harassed and belittled.

This is not the image of the heroic headteacher-leader I have in mind, or indeed wish to commend. On the other hand, neither am I entirely at ease with those conceptions of school leadership which, in the course of elaborating and applauding its dispersed nature, underplay the importance of particular individuals exercising courage on behalf of others as they go about their work. Such assimilation is likely to entail something of the kind mentioned by Aristotle in the *Poetics*, where he writes of the leader-hero as someone who is 'bigger than life' – being above the common level, possessing greater powers, greater dignity and a greater soul. Leaders of this kind, however, must still have some of the qualities of ordinary mortals, so that those over whom they have authority are able to recognize aspects of who they are in what they say and do, and are not simply overwhelmed. What sets them apart from the rest of us, however, is their boundless enthusiasm, tenacity and ingenuity, exemplified in their ability heroically to articulate, champion and mobilize commitment to a particular vision of how things should be done.

One of the ways of enhancing the morale of teachers is through the process known in the education management literature as 'developing a shared vision' – that is to say, an expression of the central values, beliefs and aims of their school, providing a 'mental picture of [its] preferred future' (Caldwell and Spinks 1992, p. 37). Where it has been agreed among staff as a whole – rather than imposed on them from above – such a vision has the potential to provide all concerned with a spur to positive action. In ideal circumstances, it can encourage staff to make changes in line with a common ideal for the evolution of the school. Crucial in this process is the progressive nature of the vision that needs to be at least one step ahead of reality for continuous improvement to result. This gap between 'reality as it is' and 'reality as one would like it' provides the necessary creative tension that is both a source of hope and a means of transformation. To have this effect, such visions have to be bold, optimistic and ambitious, and they must also offer a way forward. Heroic school leaders are often very good at being visionary in this way, and that is why I think they are needed.

While getting things in good order is probably a necessary condition for achieving organizational change, it is never sufficient. As the importance of vision-building illustrates, radical organizational change within schools is as much about the way managers and the managed *think and work together* as about the way the organization officially operates and is formally structured. What this means is that the method by which radical change is achieved organizationally must be firmly rooted in a cultural re-evaluation of the shared assumptions and beliefs which help to reproduce what goes on in a school. The interplay between the concepts and belief systems with which the staff of a school think and the social relations to which these give rise in actual fact structure their perceptions of what is practicable and appropriate. To that extent, the culture of a school sets the stage on which continuous valuations of what is possible are made. These evaluations are in significant part based upon how teachers think of themselves professionally and the ways in which their leaders reinforce and challenge the perceptions they have of what they can and cannot do.

The implications of this for the management of organizational change in schools is clear enough. Changing schools – improving them, no less – cannot just be about making adjustments to their structures, though this is part of it. It is also about *changing the people* who work in them, specifically the values and outlooks of the academic staff, which, together, help to constitute the sense they have of themselves *as teachers* and what therefore they are capable of achieving. This suggests that, in orchestrating school improvement, considerable attention needs to be focused on finding ways of helping all concerned to celebrate, evaluate and, where necessary, revise the basic ideas they think and act with. And it is often the heroic school leader who is best placed to set this process in motion and keep it under way.

Heroic optimism and school management

Anyone who has been a member of a sports team will recall with enthusiasm the role a good captain plays in enabling inspirational performance. Such individuals are able to lift the spirits of their teams on specific occasions through the exercise and sharing of optimism, even when this may be unwarranted. Certainly, good captains are not ones that admit defeat in advance of competition. They may privately think the odds are stacked against victory, but they act publicly in front of the rest of the team as if this is still a possibility. Similarly, even when defeat is staring the team in the face, and even when the final result goes badly against it, the good captain seeks to maintain morale and encourage the idea of 'living to fight another day'. Such captaincy is heroically optimistic.

Such heroic optimism, as reflected in the work of effective school leaders, takes a variety of guises. First, it is represented by a form of *infectious enthusiasm*, resulting in the individuals concerned never being defeatist in the face of difficulty. Second, such leaders are solution-driven managers, rather than problem-preoccupied ones, having consequently high personal professional expectations which they translate into a positive view of the potential and capability of everyone else. Indeed, such leaders hold very high expectations *for others*, consciously seeking out ways of reinforcing what they can do rather than drawing unnecessary attention to their shortcomings. Such leaders are thus optimists of the will, continuously drawing attention to and acknowledging publicly the achievements of staff, while seeking out ways better to tap into their potential for growth and development. Such leaders speak *with* staff, not *about or to* them, affirming their worth and encouraging their efforts, using the 'we' much more than the 'I'. Thus, unlike the worst kind of heroic leaders, they are neither dogmatic nor magisterial, preferring to influence the course of events through positive invitations and the enabling of other people's good intentions.

Farsightedness, even so, remains an aspect of such heroic endorsement.

School leaders that possess it keep asking 'Why not?' and 'What next?' Rather than collude with the idea that what is currently needed in schools is a period of stability, such leaders subscribe to the notion that change is an inevitable feature of the educational world that has to be anticipated and managed. As a result, they encourage risk-taking and experimentation among staff, while keeping a watchful eye on any negative consequences of their enthusiasms. Such leaders also recognize that they must sometimes protect their staff from the worst effects of external reforms, or see them through the pressures these often bring about. Consequently, such leaders are not afraid to be decisive when others may be unsure of how best to proceed. Such resoluteness, however, can only be exercised legitimately when there exists sufficient trust between leaders and those whom they seek to lead. In fact, trust is a necessary condition for bringing about change in any organization. Its absence fosters states of mind antithetical to taking risks and thinking and acting differently; in particular, lack of trust fosters cynicism and suspicion. Hence trust is one of the premises of the kind of heroic optimistic school leadership being argued for here. For such leaders not only act with integrity, but they also assume others behave in concert with the organization's agreed mission.

A lesson from the Romantics about heroism

At the start of her excellent compendium of biographies of heroic individuals, Hughes-Hallett observes that 'the idea of the hero would not be so emotionally disturbing or so politically dangerous were it not so potent' (2004, p. 4). The dangers are only too obvious, which means that every effort must be made to ensure they are avoided. Education has no need of modern-day Napoleons, or of other illiberal people who have equally frightening delusions of grandeur. On the other hand, there surely is no shame in acknowledging that education may need periodically some inspiration, and that heroic ways of acting in and thinking about the educational context may be helpful in providing it – for teachers and their pupils, and for school leaders. By assimilating the heroic into their pedagogic work, teachers, for example, may be better able specifically to provide pupils with excellent means for considering themselves as learner-heroes, thus increasing their confidence to take risks in their studies and in their lives generally. Much the same applies to how a school is managed, since the heroism which effective headteachers and other leaders are able to exemplify, through being enthusiastic and optimistic on behalf of beleaguered colleagues, is likely to encourage them to find new ways to overcome and transcend the difficulties they face in their professional lives. But this of course is not all that is required. For, while heroism may be a crucial factor in fostering productive pupil learning, sound pedagogy and good school management, it is, ultimately, neither necessary nor sufficient, nor equivalent to the transformative power of the creative imagination, the refinement of which is a key aim of effective teaching, as I will seek to demonstrate in the next chapter.

6

Pedagogy and the Romantic Imagination

Reason, at its height, cannot attain complete grasp and a self-contained assurance. It must fall back upon imagination – upon the embodiment of ideas in emotionally charged sense.

(*John Dewey*)

Imagination, adaptability and agency

Effective pedagogy requires teachers to possess not only the capacity and willingness to be loving and heroic but also the ability to realize unusual and productive approaches to teaching and learning that help pupils to increase their imaginative capacities. Indeed, to seek to stimulate and develop pupils in this way is arguably an aim for education to which all right-minded teachers should enthusiastically subscribe; it may also be a prerequisite to making much of what they do in the classroom educational (Egan and Nadaner 1988, p. ix).

While the imagination is commonly thought of as an aspect of the private 'inner' mental world of an individual, it is in fact indivisible from the public 'outer' one within which people exist and which, through their actions, they routinely socially reproduce. Another way of putting this is to say that efficacy and imagination are inextricably linked. Indeed, being able imaginatively to speculate forwards from reality as presently perceived – to 'unconceal future possibilities in present actualities' (Garrison 1997, p. 177) – so as to anticipate a future and altered state of affairs is a necessary condition for making new and better plans of action. Accordingly, the development of children's imaginations, both in and out of the classroom, must be one of the surest means of helping them to acquire sufficient personal agency to engage purposively with their lives, leading them to feel more in control of their destinies rather than passive victims of events and circumstances orchestrated by others. The philosopher Mary Warnock argues along similar lines: 'it is the main purpose of education to give [pupils] the opportunity ... [to learn how successfully to resist] succumbing to a feeling of futility, or to the belief that they have come to an end of what is worth having' (1976, p. 203).

Being confidently imaginative, otherwise expressed as being able to think and act resourcefully in ways that go beyond the immediately and routinely apparent, seems to me to be an important condition for achieving this. Resourcefulness of this kind is bound up with two specific qualities of the imagination. The first is an openness of mind, interpreted by me as a willingness to be receptive to new ideas and new situations. The second is the ability to transfer knowledge acquired in one context to another in order to solve problems. Taken together, these qualities of the imagination contribute positively to the growth of personal adaptability and autonomy, resulting in people being less reliant on others to help them to make sense of experience and their lives generally. If this is acceptable, then the bond between being educated and possessing a strong imagination must be a deep-rooted, even obvious, one. Knowledge of the early history of imagination as an English word, however, indicates that contemporary usage represents a radical inversion of how it was once thought of.

Imagination and the Good

While an identity or close association, entailing a consistently positive reference, exists today between education and imagination, the etymological trajectory of these two terms indicates that this is a relatively recent convergence of meaning. This reveals 'education' enjoying a consistently good reputation after it first came to regular prominence in the English language in the sixteenth century, with 'imagination' leading in the same period a somewhat equivocal existence. So, from a study of common usage, extending over nearly 500 years of English history, beginning in the first half of the fourteenth century and lasting until the advent of the Romantic period, we learn that it had very shifty, occasionally trivial, sometimes even derogatory meanings. Such interpretations were sanctioned by Holy Scripture, no less. In the Authorized Version of the Bible, for example, we find that the English word 'imagination' is used pejoratively to translate three different Hebrew words in the Old Testament and a similar number of Greek ones in the New, carrying in each case the implication that thinking and acting imaginatively is unacceptable to God, and therefore should be eliminated from people's thoughts and behaviour (McIntyre 1987, p. 5). More benignly, the early history of imagination elsewhere links its functions with fanciful thinking, being negatively contrasted with 'reason', which was regarded by far as the superior human faculty of the two. In fact, it took the Romantics, and Coleridge and Wordsworth in particular, to reconcile them, with the latter declaiming in *The Prelude* that the imagination is the 'clearest insight and amplitude of mind ... [being] ... *reason in her most exalted mood*' (Book 14, 191–2, my emphasis).

Romanticism's bringing together of these terms, however, does nothing to dilute the imagination's culturally and historically relative status. As Sutton-Smith (1988) tells us, the imagination has always been tightly harnessed to the needs of particular groups, whose evaluations of it are inevitably located in time and space. Thus, what is rightly regarded as an act of imagination in the past may not necessarily indicate imagination in people today. It follows too that the imagination is not something that is always 'good' by definition, or even in particular cases worthy of replication generally. Accordingly, while imaginative people are more likely, as Barrow observes, to be individuals with 'special insight, subtlety and farsightedness' (1988, p. 85), this does not mean that every exercise of the imagination is worthy of praise. Indeed, some imaginative thoughts and acts are clearly both wrongheaded and wrong by nature, like those devoted to securing evil rather than just or other positive objectives.

The ends of education, then again, have an ethically superior character, pointing up not only pedagogical relations that exemplify a deep respect for pupils as persons, but also the encouragement of imaginative acts on their part which typify and seek out the Good and the beautiful, including the Truth. For that reason, the cultivation by teachers of children's imaginations, in the course of seeking to *educate* them, can only be designed to bring about interpretations of the world, and actions within it, that are recognizably valuable and praiseworthy.

But, having said that, it is not easy to make out immediately either Goodness or beauty, least of all Truth, as self-evident qualities in much of current state-mandated educational practice. On the contrary, central to government policy for schools in the UK today are dogmatic pronouncements about 'standards', 'efficiency', 'choice' and 'diversity', collectively associated with regulatory edicts that prescribe curriculum content and pupil-attainment targets, each backed up by high-stakes testing and other associated managerial emphases, including performance league-tables. Together, such policies, which are rarely supported or informed by credible evidence, blunt and dishearten, rather than sharpen and encourage, teachers' ability to look imaginatively beyond things as they are (towards, in other words, new conceptions in education of the Good and beautiful), thus compromising their best efforts to foster equivalent forms of creativity among the pupils they teach.

In view of that, it becomes all the more necessary for teachers to exercise and develop professionally their own pedagogic imaginations, so as better to nurture the creative potential of their pupils. The Romantics are well equipped to facilitate this outcome, chiefly because their huge intellectual legacy includes a profound understanding of the nature of the life of the imagination. Warnock argues that '[i]t is impossible to understand the concept of the imagination without attempting to understand [their version of it] ... [Indeed] ... there is some sense in which [the Romantics'] ... version is true, and fits the facts' (1976, p. 201). Moreover, studying what they say about it is a helpful way to restore to critical consciousness some of the central organizing ideas of progressive forms of teaching and learning which have been lost to teachers' professional thinking and practice in recent years as a result of the school reforms identified earlier. Revisiting what the Romantics say about the importance of the imaginative life might also be the first stage in facilitating among them the identification of an alternative vision of schooling that eschews the retrospective, routine and uniform character of recent government education policy in favour of something more expansive and exhilarating.

Joy, truth and usurpation

Coleridge and Wordsworth together, and Hazlitt independently, attempted serious, complex definitions of the imagination. It is as though they each experienced their creativity so strongly that they felt a huge urge to make sense of it as something above and beyond their own literary output.

Given the intricacy and the quantity of what they each wrote on the imagination, where should one begin in analysing their contribution and assessing its importance for the practice of education? The initial recalling of a piece of philosophical history, followed by more detailed scrutiny of specifics relevant to the educational purposes of this book, is my preferred intellectual route map.

No adequate appreciation of the Romantics' understanding of the nature of the imagination, particularly in the case of Coleridge, is complete without knowing that many of its most significant aspects took their intellectual cues from German idealist thought, and Immanuel Kant's psychological theory of cognition in particular. Unlike the English eighteenth-century scientific concept of 'seeing' as a sort of objective photographic record of reality, Kant's theory, chiefly set down in his

Critique of Judgement (1790), acknowledges the subjective role of the imagination, privileging the capacity we have simultaneously to make mental images, pictures or representations of raw sense data and to *translate* them into a world of objects that exists independently of ourselves, having the stamp on them of our personal psychologies, memories and previous experience. In bridging the gap theoretically between sensation and intelligible thought, Kant's conception of the imagination sought to make sense of that faculty of mind which enables people to create another nature out of the very material that actual nature gives them in the first place through experience.

Coleridge knew well Kant's analysis, including its philosophical detail, having studied and been heavily influenced by it during his European travels. Indeed, he was, if not singlehandedly, at least significantly, responsible for bringing it to the attention of his intellectual peers and friends in this country, including of course Wordsworth, and maybe Hazlitt as well. As Warnock says: 'Coleridge was the vehicle for the introduction of German philosophy into England and ... the theory of the imagination to be found in his work contains features which ... seem to contribute to a true view of the imaginative function' (1976, p. 73). This view sought to achieve two objectives: first, to establish *theoretically* what the imagination does; and, second, to describe how it works *in practice* – that is to say, to define imagination as *both* a psychological theory and a literary method.

While students of the philosophy of mind and English literature can usually be easily interested in the fine-grain detail of Coleridge's thesis on the nature of the creative imagination, its application specifically to the practice of education, I readily admit, is not immediately apparent, suggesting that teachers may not have much, if anything, to learn from it. Closer inspection, however, suggests otherwise, particularly when one considers Coleridge's account of what the imaginative function entails and facilitates. There are two connected aspects to this – one has to do with joy; the other with Truth.

Coleridge's psychology of the imagination's importance embodies a view about its role in fostering feelings of *joy*, linked with a general liveliness of mind, bordering sometimes on a form of thrilling erotic ecstasy, which in every instance derives from people experiencing, through its application, a recognizably improved sense of perceiving more than is immediately apparent; or of appreciating events differently and better; or of being active in ways previously unanticipated, but now gladly undertaken. Wordsworth's poetics of the unconscious articulate here, particularly when he draws attention to the way in which exercises of the creative imagination have the capacity to take us over, condensing thought to either a passion or an extraordinary enlivened sense of reality, or both. Jonathan Wordsworth, the contemporary literary scholar who, until his recent death, specialized in the work of his poetic ancestor, calls this kind of losing oneself a form of 'imaginative usurpation' (Wordsworth 1982, pp. 174–202), illustrating it by quoting different parts of *The Prelude* in which Wordsworth himself actually uses this notion metaphorically:

> I looked about, and lo
> The moon stood naked in the heavens at height
> Immense above my head, and on the shore
> I found myself of a huge sea of mist
> Which meek and silent rested at my feet.
> . . .
> In headlands, tongues, and promontory shapes
> Into the sea, the real sea, that seemed
> To dwindle and give up its majesty
> *Usurped upon as far as sight could reach.*
>   (*The Prelude*, Book 13, 40–51, my emphasis)

> Imagination! – lifting up itself
> Before the eye and the progress of my song
> Like an unfathered vapour, here that power
> In all the might of its endowments, came
> Athwart me. I was lost as in a cloud
> Halted without a struggle, to break through
> And now, recovering, to my soul I say
> 'I recognise thy glory'. In such strength
> *Of usurpation, in such visitings*
> Of awful promise, when the light of sense
> Goes out in flashes that have shewn to us
> The invisible world, doth greatness make abode
> There harbours whether we be young or old.
>   (Book 6, 525–37, my emphasis)

Classroom learning experiences that realize such states should surely interest any teacher. Indeed, teachers' own imaginative pedagogic practices are likely to have parallel effects on themselves, leading to increases in their job-satisfaction and sense of professional well-being generally. The principle is a simple one: pupils make more effective learners if what they are encouraged to learn illuminates for the better –

and distractedly – their experience of being schooled; and teaching becomes more effective if those that practise it have maximum opportunity to look for, find and enjoy creative solutions to how best to interest and motivate pupils.

Contrary feelings, such as being bored, or being overly controlled, in each case, diminish efficacy, frustrating effective teaching and learning as a result. Of course, the feelings of joy that one might experience from teaching well or learning effectively need to be kept in proportion and perspective. To be sure, they do not offer an ultimate justification for teaching and learning in a particular way. Something similar has been said about making 'the pursuit of happiness' an aim for education (see Dearden 1972, for example). For while no good teacher would question whether or not happiness is valuable, in the sense that teaching in ways that promote it is likely to be educationally beneficial, this does not mean that for learning to be 'effective' it must always be associated with pleasant feelings. On the contrary, such learning may require personal struggle, which for some pupils, and the rest of us, cannot always be harmonized with short-term personal happiness. But analysing happiness in this way does not undermine the case I am seeking to make here, which is not about elevating the achievement of joy to the status of an educational aim, but rather about recognizing how particular forms of pedagogy that stress the imaginative function in children's experience of learning are capable of realizing for them feelings of greater efficacy, linked with a positive sense of experiencing and understanding things in new ways which delight the mind and encourage a distracted optimism of spirit.

I can best explain further what I am getting at here by referring directly to Coleridge, and specifically to Warnock's (1976) discussion of his contrarily titled ode, 'Dejection', written in 1802, in which the poet seeks to communicate the miserable feelings he is experiencing, having temporarily lost touch with his imaginative powers.

Having described the night sky – its stars and crescent moon – Coleridge, Warnock reminds us, writes this:

> I see them all so excellently fair
> I see, not feel, how beautiful they are.
>
> My general spirits fail;
> And what can these avail
> To lift the smothering weight from off my breast?
> It were a vain endeavour
> Though I should gaze for ever

> On that green light that lingers in the west;
> I may not hope from outward forms to win
> The passions and the life, whose fountains are within ...
>
> There was a time when though my path was rough
> This joy within me dallied with distress
> And all misfortunes were but as the stuff
> Whence fancy made me dreams of happiness:
>
> For hope grew round me, like the twining vine,
> And fruits and foliage, not my own, seemed mine.
> But now afflictions bow me down to earth
> Nor care I that they rob me of my mirth;
> But oh each visitation
> Suspends what nature gave me at my birth
> My shaping spirit of imagination.
>
> (Richards 1978, pp. 170–2)

The lessening of Coleridge's imaginative capacities means he 'sees' without 'feeling'; and 'gazes' without 'passion'. He is 'bowed down' as a result, being 'robbed' of 'mirth' and 'joy', each the product of his current failure to 'shape' his experience of the external world in ways previously enjoyed.

The imagination's power to combine – to bring together ideas and sensations so as to create an external reality that causes in us feelings of joy, awe and love – is central to Coleridge's appreciation of its nature and significance, the absence of which contributes directly to the despair he suffers as a result of being unable to be creative in ways previously enjoyed. The imagination, he writes, is a 'shaping and modifying power' that blends, fuses and harmonizes the 'thoughts and passions of man into every thing which is the object of his contemplation ... stamping them into unity in the mould of a moral idea' (*Biographia Literaria*, chapter 13). These are crucial insights, pointing us towards an appreciation of the selective, synoptic and integrative functions of the imagination: it selects from the mass of material with which the senses are confronted, concentrating on their most significant features; then it proceeds to synthesize the material around it and in terms of it, drawing everything into a systematic unity.

The imagination in Coleridge's scheme is not only a primary source of discernment and a means better to integrate experience. It is also the faculty that is the most truly active aspect of creative thinking generally, its distinguishing characteristic being *originality*, the feature that gives it its *divine* quality, being a 'repetition of God's eternal act of creation' (*Biographia Literaria*, chapter 13). The imagination's divine attributes realize for those who exercise it fully a world, therefore, of greater meaning than is accessible to the mere senses. In other words, the imagination has an interpretative function which is fulfilled through its capacity to observe analogous connections between entities, chiefly because it is sensitive to, and perceptive of, features in the world and in persons which less perceptive intellects accidentally miss or overlook altogether. As Bowra states: 'So far from thinking the imagination deals with the non-existent, the Romantics believe that, when it is at work, it sees things to which the ordinary intelligence is blind and that it is intimately connected with a special insight or perception or intuition' (1961, p. 7).

This 'special insight' is a version of the *Truth* – a reality ordinarily masked by visible things that only the imagination is capable of uncovering. This truth acts as a reflecting mirror of the *meaning of all things*, revealing their order and unfathomable depths. Bowra again:

> The Romantics ... agreed that their task was to find through the imagination some transcendental order which explains the world of appearances and accounts ... for the existence of visible things ... They were metaphysicians who trusted not in logic but in insight, not in the analytical reason, but in the delighted inspired soul ... [who] attempted to discover the world of spirit through the unaided efforts of the soul.
>
> (Bowra 1961, pp. 22–3)

Stripped of these quasi-religious features, what we have here is a view about the cognitive role that the imagination plays in our intellectual lives, aiding the development of knowledge and understanding – of ourselves, of other people, and of the world – which would otherwise remain beyond our ken. To that extent, to repeat what I said at the start of this chapter, the Romantics teach us that the imagination is not a private aspect of a person's mind. Rather it is the means whereby a public world is created by interacting and creative individuals who, by thinking in sufficient social harmony, realize enough intersubjective agreement about the nature of things and feelings to, so to speak, bring them into existence.

Wordsworth's *Tintern Abbey*

Many of the features of the imagination to which Coleridge draws our attention – its selective, synoptic, integrative and interpretative functions – are taken up and given special emphases in the poetry and other writings of Wordsworth, which is not surprising given the close intellectual and artistic collaboration and friendship that existed between them (Sisman 2006). As Heffernan says: 'Wordsworth's definition of imagination is substantially the same as that of Coleridge' (1969, p. 189), any difference between them being less about substance and more about origins. For while Coleridge's understanding of the imagination was mostly developed intellectually, Wordsworth's grew out of his experience, including especially examination of what it was he was doing in writing poetry and seeking to achieve generally as a writer.

Of pivotal significance here is Wordsworth's great autobiographical poem, *Lines written a few miles above Tintern Abbey*, written in 1798 during a return visit to the Wye Valley and published shortly afterwards as the last item in *Lyrical Ballads*. As he said: 'No poem of mine was composed under circumstances more pleasant for me to remember than this' (Barker 2000, p. 155). No other poem of Wordsworth's either sets down in such clear terms his distinctive view of nature – its sublime spiritual presence – and the role of the imagination in this new vision, including, crucially for my purposes at this point, the manner in which it helps people to make sense of time and its passing in the process of the construction of identity.

The imagination, Wordsworth suggests in *Tintern Abbey*, allows us to treat the past as if it were present by reliving the experience of it as if it were so, encouraging continuity in how we think of ourselves as people with distinctive personal identities. As Blades observes, this poem, probably more than any other that Wordsworth wrote, is 'vitally concerned with the theme of "becoming" ... It is a poem rich in the nuances and scales of time' (Blades 2004, p. 56). Gill, one of Wordsworth's contemporary biographers, agrees, stating that *Tintern Abbey* is 'shaped by the activity of mind determined to generate from the past energy for the present and future' (Gill 1989, p. 152). This famous passage from it is foundational:

> ... Once again
> Do I behold these steep and lofty cliffs,
> Which on a wild secluded scene impress
> Thought of more deep seclusion; and connect
> The landscape with the quiet of the sky ...

Though absent long
These forms of beauty have not been to me
As is a landscape to a blind man's eye:
But oft in lonely rooms, and, mid the din
Of towns and cities, I have owed to them
In hours of weariness sensations sweet,
Felt in the blood and felt along the heart,
And passing even into my purer mind
With tranquil restoration ...
Nor less, I trust,
To them I may have owed another gift
Of aspect more sublime; that blessed mood
In which the burthen of the mystery,
In which the heavy and the weary weight
Of all this unintelligible world
Is lighten'd: that serene and blessed mood
In which the affections lead us on,
Until, the breath of this corporeal frame,
And even the motion of our human blood
Almost suspended, we are laid asleep
In body, and become a living soul:
While with an eye made quiet by the power
Of harmony and the deep power of joy,
We see into the life of things.

(Tintern Abbey, 15–49)

The mention at the end of 'joy' of course is something we might expect, given my highlighting of this sensation earlier on. More subtle is the manner in which Wordsworth emphasizes the power of the imagination to recollect images and feelings long after they were first experienced – 'Though absent long'.

Such recollected emotion, which is a leitmotif in Wordsworth's theory of the imagination, is restorative ('Felt in the blood and felt along the heart / And passing even into my purer mind / With tranquil restoration'), leading to an understanding of the 'life of things', making it possible to perceive a deeper, richer reality in and through them. The direct experience of nature, Wordsworth suggests, is not sufficient to bring this about; also required is the 'mind's imaginative eye', which enables us, through selection, synopsis and association, to concentrate upon those images which are most meaningful to us, reliving past experience in the present, and in more powerful and vivid ways. Wordsworth explains that this imaginative re-enactment facilitates a 'sense sublime' that allows one to see 'something far more deeply infused'. As Blades remarks: 'Here this visionary dimension has enabled [Wordsworth] to see beyond the [recollected] beauties of the pastoral scene of the Wye, to understand the spiritual and moral forces in nature; but, further, to understand the relationship between these forces, the objects in nature and his own powerful imagination' (2004, p. 52).

McIntyre also aids our understanding at this juncture. His interpretation of the importance of the role imaginative images play in knowledge, communication and emotion is linked to an effort that Wordsworth would have appreciated his namely, to create a theological understanding of the relationship between religious faith and the functions of the imagination. Among the 13 positive particulars of such image-making which McIntyre itemizes, one is especially relevant to the present discussion. This emphasizes the 'sustentative' role of images, by which McIntyre means their capacity to help keep us going in the face of a flagging faith and a fading conviction: 'No matter our denominational loyalty, we all depend heavily on the sustentative power of images, not because they have any power in themselves, but because they have been in our lives the means whereby God has so constantly refreshed and renewed us' (1987, p. 174).

This is precisely what Wordsworth means when he writes of the restorative power of those of his recollected emotions first prompted when revisiting the Wye Valley. This encourages a related question, for our purposes: what pedagogical images might similarly help and motivate teachers to teach better when their morale is low and encourage forms of effective learning among dispirited pupils frustrated and bowed down by persistent failure? For sure, they are likely to include recollections of successful teaching and learning – stories, say, featuring both teacher and taught overcoming, heroically even, and together, a problem that previously had proved very difficult to resolve. Such images, which need to be positive in character, avoiding all intimations of guilt, would also be ones that foster a sense of personal worth, emphasizing an individual's strengths rather than weaknesses.

They might also seek to challenge the negative images frequently, and improperly, associated by some teachers with children from poor home backgrounds, including those belonging to ethnic minority families, whose educational careers often suffer from their self-fulfilling prophecies which condemn them to failure before they even get started. The restorative or sustaining power of images makes them, by turn, 're-creative', providing a basis, among others, for teachers and pupils to learn more effectively together, either again, or for the first time, working more profitably – more lovingly – with each other than was previously possible.

Making a valued absence present in this way cannot ever be a bad thing, either in life generally or in teaching and learning contexts in particular. Indeed, Hazlitt's important theory of the imagination, to which we now turn for additional illumination, is based on an interesting inversion of this principle, suggesting that a key function of the imaginative life is not so much to recreate the past as to enter into the future, including, empathetically, the lives of other people. While the more obvious implications of this last claim for pedagogy are immediately apparent, we need to delve into Hazlitt's theory of mind in more detail, so as to appreciate better its greater relevance for teaching and learning.

Sympathetic and disinterested benevolence

Hazlitt was intellectually and emotionally opposed to the abstract application of closed systems of thought, whether empirical or metaphysical, to those aspects of human experience where he believed they did not belong, which for him were the majority. Indeed, for Hazlitt, abstraction of almost any kind constituted the gravest threat to the quality of people's response to life, and to the timbre of civilized living generally, which, he argued, can only be engaged with meaningfully via feeling, passion and sensibility. Feeling, and only feeling, in his view, is capable of capturing the evanescent complexity of nature, living and art: 'In art, in taste, in life ... you decide from feeling, and not from reason' (Wu 1998, Vol. 6, p. 26). Feelings thus always direct thought: 'I say what I think: I think what I feel' (Wu 1998, Vol. 3, p. 5).

Hazlitt's assessment of the primacy of feeling and his attack on abstraction were first developed in his schooldays in Hackney, during which time he first encountered and began to critique the so-called 'modern philosophers' of his time – in particular, John Locke and his theory of mind. The philosophical detail of Hazlitt's critique, which is set down formally in his *Essay on the Principles of Human Action* (published much later in 1805 when he was 27 years old) is impressive by any of today's academic standards. It is also, as Grayling remarks (2000, p. 92), a difficult and complex read, entirely devoid of the sort of literary flourishes and forms of plain speaking that became Hazlitt's trademark and eventual legacy. In attempting to summarize his *Essay*, which is all I intend to do here, I am conscious of simplifying and possibly even trivializing what Hazlitt considered to be his major contribution to thought – indeed one that infused and motivated all his subsequent writings and by which he wished them therefore to be judged. (On this claim, and others about the book, see Park 1971; Albrecht 1965; Mahoney 1981; Bromwich 1999; Nataragan 1998; Grayling 2000 and Natarajan *et al.* 2005.).

The central thesis of the *Essay* is that the human mind is simultaneously 'sympathetically disinterested' and 'autonomously creative'. It is 'sympathetically disinterested' in the sense that people, according to Hazlitt, are not inherently selfishly motivated but rather as sympathetically interested in the welfare of others as in their own happiness; it is 'autonomously creative' in the sense that it is the imaginative master and not – as Locke would have us believe – the mechanistic slave of sense impressions. The first part of this couplet is the more difficult one to appreciate, for it flies in the face of those elements of common sense that suggest that the fundamental motivation for people's actions is nearly always self-interest and only very rarely the interests of others. Hazlitt's detailed defence of his contrary position is grounded in the idea that we can only rationally pursue and seek to construct the form and content of *future* states of affairs – the past and actually occurring present each being out of our influence and control. And because the future does not exist, there is in strict truth nothing to pursue selfishly in it. Indeed, for Hazlitt, even our own identities do not strictly exist at any one moment in time inasmuch as they have to be continuously recreated almost from scratch, despite impressions and habits of thought which suggest the opposite. As Bromwich says on Hazlitt's behalf: 'We cannot be affected by something we have never felt; we have never felt the effect of a future event; we cannot therefore act mechanically with respect to the future: [rather] we must act imaginatively [in the present]' (Bromwich 1983, p. 52).

In acting in the present to reconstruct ourselves, we are, says Hazlitt, compelled anew to imagine disinterestedly what our prospective personal and corporate identities might be like. This process, he insists, logically requires us to think about and take into account not just our own self but other selves as well – to possess a form of *sympathy* that allows us to project, to enter into another reality and to share its being, and thus to create a future free of the the limitations of past and present feelings and practice – a mode of sensibility which he might say compels teachers to underplay the background of pupils in judging their capacity to learn. It could also, as I will indicate later, provide an optimistic foundation for the very practice of teaching. As Hazlitt says:

> The imagination, by means of which alone I can anticipate future objects, or be interested in them, must carry me out of myself into the

feelings of others by one and the same process by which I am thrown forward as it were into my future being, and interest in it. I could not love myself, if I were not capable of loving others. Self-love, used in this sense, is in its fundamental principle the same as disinterested benevolence.

(Wu 1998, Vol. 1, p. 3)

The practical implications of this transcendental position are far-reaching, suggesting not only that we are all perfectly capable of living fully moral lives, but also that, to do so, we must act creatively – imaginatively and immediately – on ourselves, other people and the world in order to fashion disinterestedly a credible future at both the individual and social level. On this understanding, to borrow Paulin's words, the imagination, in Hazlitt's scheme, is always 'essentially and benignly social' (1998, p. 35). McIntyre labels this the 'empathic' function of imagination: 'the way in which it is able to project us not only intellectually into deeper understanding of a situation, but also effectively and emotionally into it, so that we identify with its components and with the persons involved in it' (McInbyre 1987, p. 162). Moreover, because situations and people are never, according to Hazlitt, the same for two moments together, the synoptic and integrative capacities of the imagination act as the primary means whereby we make sense of who we are in the world at any one moment, and of our actions within it, as these affect both people and things.

Mary Warnock's study of the imagination (from which I have already quoted) supports this, concluding that 'there would be no world to be understood without a prior imaginative construction [of it]' (Warnock 1987, p. 71). Although she does not refer to Hazlitt, Warnock's analysis is similar to his in one other significant way: the manner in which, like him, she describes the imagination as a *power* in the human mind, impelled by *passionate fervour*, that

enables us to see the world, whether present or absent, as significant, and also to present this vision to others, for them to share and reject. And *this power ... is not only intellectual. Its impetus comes from the emotions as much as from the reason, from the heart as much as from the head.*

(Warnock 1987, p. 196, my emphasis)

Hazlitt himself could have written these words, for they precisely convey his view that the full and proper exercise of our rational capacities cannot ever be just a cold, dry, matter-of-fact process, but rather must be an imaginative, indeed passionate, one. He makes this last point in a telling way in his critique of weak orators: 'Modesty, impartiality and candour are not the virtues of a public speaker. He must be confident, inflexible, uncontrollable, overcoming all oppositions by his ardour and impetuosity ... Calm inquiry, sober truth, and speculative indifference, will never carry any point' (Wu 1998, 4, p. 278). With hindsight, and our knowledge of twentieth-century demagoguery, we may overstep the mark thinking that Hazlitt is here. Even so, it is a reminder of the importance of recognizing a positive role for passion and emotion in rational deliberation. There is also a suggestion here about the nature of the creative impulse and of its psychological consequences, which Mahoney describes in these terms:

> Strong passion triggers the imagination to seek and struggle for a mode of embodying the sometimes wild and indistinct cravings of the mind and will. The basic concern of the imagination is not with things as they are, but rather with things as they are touched by the *peculiar electricity of our psychic lives*. At times, only the imagination, with its wondrous powers, can begin to match the infinitely varied responses evoked by the power of human passion; only the imagination can reveal a thing as it is felt to exist and as a human is compelled to think of it.
>
> (Mahoney 1981, p. 106, my emphasis)

Pedagogy, butterflies and bullets

Hazlitt unhesitatingly and unequivocally pins his life's work and his vision for humankind on the power of the creative imagination, which he sees as the means by which people forge meaningful and credible personal identities and by which they translate thought, feeling and sensation into moral actions. Consequently, he is particularly impatient with those whose actions would inhibit the creative imagination, and therefore lead to abstractionism rather than sympathetic wholeness.

Thus, while one could imagine Hazlitt welcoming education's current preoccupation with finding new ways to promote 'creativity' in school classrooms, he would, I am sure, be horrified by the context in which this is expected to be achieved – a context in which teaching is increasingly subjected to performance forms of management, and learning to cut-and-dried attainment targets. He would surely regard such abstractionism as the antithesis of education.

For Hazlitt, genuine learning (as we saw earlier) comes instead from an imaginative combination of reading and observation of life. It certainly does not derive from a school curriculum grounded in certain predefined and decontextualized 'basic skills', least of all in teaching centrally prescribed subjects that are not comprehensively linked with the lives of pupils who are expected to be initiated into them. Such forms of disassociated book-learning, according to Hazlitt, always lead to ignorant and uneducated states of mind. He cynically makes this point in a series of ironic observations about an individual who clearly reads a lot, but whose judgement has been hardly tutored for the better as a result:

> Such a one may be said to carry his understanding about with him in his pocket, or to leave it at home on his library shelves. He is afraid of venturing on any train of reasoning, or of striking out any observation that is not mechanically suggested to him by passing his eyes over certain legible characters ... He has no ideas of his own, and must live off other people ... He knows as much of what he talks about as a blind man does of colours ... He is expert in all the dead and in most of the living languages; but he can neither speak his own fluently, nor write it correctly.
>
> (Wu 1998, Vol. 6, p. 61)

Similar sentiments are expressed by Hazlitt in his advice to his young son, William, on the occasion of his departure to boarding school: 'You will bring with you from your books and solitary reveries a wrong measure of men and things, unless you correct it by careful experience and mixed observation' (Howe, 17, p. 87).

Indeed, Hazlitt is persuaded that 'expertise' (what today we might define as abstract intellectualism) is better replaced by a form of 'common sense' that is uninfluenced by 'schooling', or any kind of formal education for that matter – an attitude that may provide the reason for his apparent lack of interest in educational issues to do with provision and access, suggesting also that he was a 'de-schooler' long before this movement came into being:

> Uneducated people have most exuberance of invention and the greatest freedom from prejudice ... They argue from what they see and know, instead of spinning cobweb distinctions of what things ought to be ... You will hear more good things on the outside of a stage-coach from London to Oxford than if you were to pass a twelvemonth with the undergraduates, or heads of colleges, of that famous university; and more *home* truths are to be learnt from listening to a noisy debate in an alehouse than from attending to a formal one in the House of Commons.
>
> (Wu 1998, Vol. 6, pp. 65–6)

Once again, Hazlitt is overreaching himself here. Even so, his vivid sending-up here of the educated classes in *Table Talk*, and elsewhere, has a strong ring of truth to it. He considered the seat of knowledge and understanding to be found neither in book-learning as an end in itself nor in prescribed curricula, but instead 'in the head', by which he means 'in the imagination'. Wisdom, similarly, is located 'in the heart'. He concludes: 'we are sure to judge wrong, if we do not feel right.' (Howe 1928–32, Vol. 9, p. 222).

The idea that effective teaching can be reduced to, and measured by, competence and outcome-based strategies is, then, totally at odds with Hazlitt's conception of the educated person and of the nature of thought and action generally. Such a person, in his scheme, is someone who is true to his or her convictions, someone who does not hark continuously back to the past and follow convention for the sake of it; and someone who consequently is never dogmatic, who, as he famously puts it, 'lives in the dream of their own experience and who sees all things in the light of their own minds' – someone, in other words, who possesses and uses a strong and independent imagination.

Hazlitt's attack on Coleridge resonates here. Coleridge, he says, while possessing great 'intellectual wealth', has 'a mind [simply] reflecting ages past: his voice is like the echo of the congregated roar of the dark rearward and abyss of thought'. Meanwhile, poor Mr Gifford (editor of the Tory *Quarterly Review*) another of Hazlitt's targets,

> is in utter want of independence and magnanimity in all that he attempts. He cannot go alone; he must have crutches, a go-cart and trammels ... He cannot conceive of anything different from how he finds it, and hates those who pretend to a greater reach of intellect or boldness of spirit than himself. He inclines ... to the traditional in laws and government, to the orthodox in religion, to the safe in opinion, to the trite in imagination, to the technical in style, to whatever implies a surrender of individual judgement into the hands of authority, and a subjection of individual freedom to mechanistic rules.
>
> (Wu 1998, Vol. 7, p. 182)

Effective teaching (one could imagine Hazlitt writing) is centrally about the disinterested and imaginative pursuit of opportunities that enable learners to construct for themselves meaningful personal identities, including responses to, and reinterpretations of, their experience – of other people, of events and of circumstances generally. Hazlitt's insistence that this takes place anew during each waking moment through the exercise of the creative imagination is an idealization of what empirically is a more constrained process. For Hazlitt's theory of action must be wrong at this point, to the degree that none of us, not just teachers, is ever able entirely to escape the influence of past events and experience, or the limiting aspects of the present context. On the other hand, teachers can work hard to seek ways to avoid their compromising effects, rather than assume their negative self-fulfilling impacts. They can also embrace the idea that teaching – lesson by lesson – offers them a series of opportunities, experiments almost, to 'start all over again', as if each time from scratch, thus fostering a form of optimism about their ability to teach, despite the shockingly bad circumstances in which they are sometimes compelled to work.

It is fair to say also that Hazlitt would have hated the abstractionism, or 'second-orderliness', of those philosophers of education who have sought in times past to define teaching analytically. I suspect he would have shuddered, as I do now, at reading for example: 'Teaching is the label for those activities of a person A, the intention of which is to bring about in another person, B, the intentional learning of X.' These are the words of the eminent educational philosopher, Paul Hirst (1973, p. 172), published at the peak of the influence of London's so-called 'Bedford Way School of Philosophy of Education', of which he was a prominent exponent. While these words offer a logically coherent definition of teaching, what they say about its actual nature is unrecognizable to this former classroom teacher. Hazlitt, I guess, would prefer, and find far more illuminating, sociological, ethnographic *descriptions* of what goes in school classrooms, such as the ones expressed in the following three empirically derived extracts:

> Teachers practise an art. Moments of choice of what to do, how to do it, with whom and at what pace, arise hundreds of time a school day, and arise differently every day and with every group of students. No command or instruction can be so formulated as to control that kind of artistic judgement and behaviour.
>
> (Schwab 1983, p. 245)

> Teaching is an opportunistic process. That is to say, neither the teacher nor his students can predict with any certainty exactly what will happen next. Plans are forever going awry and unexpected opportunities for the attainment of educational goals are constantly emerging. The seasoned teacher seizes upon these opportunities and uses them to his and his students' advantage ... Although most teachers make plans in advance, they are aware as they make them of the likelihood of change ... They know, or come to know, that the path of educational progress more closely resembles the flight of a butterfly than the flight of a bullet.
>
> (Jackson 1968, pp. 166–7)

Teaching is an art in the sense that the teacher's activity is not dominated by prescriptions or routines, but is influenced by qualities and contingencies that are unpredicted ... Teaching is an art in the sense that the ends it achieves are often created in the process.

(Eisner 1979, p. 154)

Unlike Hirst's analytic definition, these vivid descriptions get to the heart of what teaching *as a form of life* is actually like. In particular, they draw attention to the way in which it involves the utilization of complex, diverse skills in real-life contexts that are unpredictable and constantly evolving. They implicitly draw attention also to what other students of teaching have stressed about its nature – the fact (despite what Hirst says about it, which is empirically wrong) that *teachers do not always know, when they are teaching, what precisely they are doing*. Rather, they often function intuitively, using in the process skills of imaginative foresight and improvisation (Atkinson and Claxton 2000; Humphreys and Hyland 2002), which makes the identification of their intentions often unclear, both to themselves and to others (including their pupils) watching them. In fact, there are occasions when good teaching follows no method except that of the personality of the teacher herself. This does not render such activity as non-teaching, however, which is what Hirst seems to be suggesting. Rather, it indicates that such activity is always pragmatic and multifarious, frequently extemporized and occasionally makeshift, indicating that a necessary condition for its improvement is more likely to come from imaginative rather than conceptual analysis.

Lessons from the Romantics about the imagination

While this chapter has ranged widely, its central arguments are easy to condense. They focus ultimately on *three theorems about the imagination*, each of which is brought into prominent focus by the Romantic impulse, reminding us simultaneously of their importance for education. Significantly, as in the case of heroism, these theories have positive implications, not only for pupils, but for teachers as well.

Theorem 1 stresses the role of the imagination in enabling teachers and pupils alike to make better sense, respectively, of their professional and learning lives. Indeed, the efficacy of both teachers and taught is enhanced in proportion to the degree to which each is able to unlock and reproduce in practice those creative abilities which realize original thoughts and actions, chiefly through their different capacities to be cognitively selective, synoptic and integrative in new ways. Accordingly, both teachers and pupils need – in order to become mature learners – recurring opportunities to acquire and develop the tools to conceptualize better how their respective lives could be made different and superior, including the inner confidence and motivation to make this happen.

For this to take place, they each need to be encouraged to take risks and to fail in self-assured ways. To do this, pupils and their teachers must find ways to enjoy learning together, and, to recall my earlier mentioning of 'imaginative usurpation', occasionally to allow themselves, jointly, to become 'lost' in the process of learning itself. This imaginative project is not simply about the arts, however. It is about questioning, making connections and inventing and reinventing in *all* subject areas. To that extent, it has to be seen as a curriculum-wide matter, though one that is worked through in ways appropriate to situation and purpose, as Barrow correctly advises: 'It cannot be seen as the business of special courses or exercises in such things as problem solving, critical thinking, or creativity, because imagination ... presupposes understanding and competence within the specific contexts in which it is displayed' (Barrow 1988, p. 90).

Theorem 2 brings to our attention the capacity of the imagination to foster greater empathetic sensibility, and thus, using Shelley's words, 'to be a great instrument of moral good'. This function is facilitated by the part imagination plays in helping people to make better sense of how they experience time, enabling them not just to treat the past as present – to relive it as if it were immediately apparent – but to embrace the future similarly, a combination of processes that provides all of us with the necessary sense of existing meaningfully and continually. However, these retrospective and anticipatory aspects of the imagination – (*Wordsworth*: 'Though absent long / These forms of beauty have not been to me / As is a landscape to a blind man's eye'; *Hazlitt*: 'I am thrown forward as it were into my own future being') – encourages more than just an increased sense of ourselves and of places and things. More importantly, it brings on an ability to feel better for and about the needs of others and the impact our actions might have in each case. That is to say, as Hazlitt advises, by projecting us emotionally into particular situations, the imagination helps us to identify most notably with the persons involved in them.

This process is a fundamental aspect of effective pedagogy, to the degree that teaching well requires its practitioners to think ahead – divine, even – how alternative courses of action will work out, both immediately and in the medium and longer term. This has practical and policy implications, as well as directly moral ones – *practical*, because it alerts teachers to the need to continue to improve their classroom craft knowledge, leading to greater intuitive sensitivity about how pupils might react to the pedagogical demands they routinely make on them; and *policy*, because it reminds school leaders to anticipate and ameliorate the unintended and sometimes negative consequences of their larger-scale decisions, some of which can have major effects on pupils' overall educational and other life chances. The trite comment made by certain education management consultants that modern school leaders need to 'think more out of the box' connects here, despite the fact that these advisers often do not understand the full implications of what they commend. Studying the nature of the imagination, and its application in the educational context, might help them to do so.

Theorem 3 is to do with the imagination's restorative aspects, which links with Wordsworth's notion of 'recollected emotion' – the facility provided by the imagination to relive and enjoy again in the present positive experiences felt in the past. As I stated earlier, to ignore the importance of such images, for both teachers and pupils, is to run a high risk indeed, particularly in learning situations in which failure and low motivation are deeply inscribed. To be sure, the recalling and retelling of positive stories of pedagogy are unlikely to be sufficient to raise significantly pupil achievement and increase teacher effectiveness and confidence. On the other hand, given the special salience which narratives of this sort have in schools – in the playground and in the staffroom – they should not be ruled out of consideration, but rather instantiated in ways other than the formal, as exemplified in the moral tales told in and out of school assemblies and prize-giving events. What is needed as well, or maybe instead, is the creation of an overall school culture of effective learning that renders such theatricality unnecessary or of lesser significance.

A fourth theorem about the imagination which might well have found expression in this chapter concerns its role in *being subversive*, a process requiring individuals creatively sometimes to turn convention on its head, daring them occasionally also to speak the truth directly to power. Because of its singular importance, manifest in the heavy weight accorded by particular Romantics to being a critic of and dissenter from contemporary social mores, I have chosen to devote the whole of the next chapter to a discussion of what it means to possess and use a radical attitude of mind, in education and generally. There I will outline a progressive prospectus for how education academics can better pursue their vocation as *public intellectuals* through becoming freshly acquainted with, and being influenced by, one of the Romantic culture-heroes whose writings and ideas are celebrated in this book – William Hazlitt.

7

Romantic Intellectualism and Persuasive Eloquence: Hazlitt and the Art of Educational Criticism

> *True teaching can be a terribly dangerous enterprise ... To teach greatly is to awaken doubts in the pupil, to train for dissent.*
>
> (*George Steiner*)

> *The Dissenter does not change his sentiments with the season; he does not suit his conscience to his convenience ... He will not give up his principles because they are unfashionable ... He speaks his mind, bluntly and honestly.*
>
> (*William Hazlitt*)

Teaching and subversion

George Steiner's idea of teachers as agents of dissent has a long history, going back to Socrates and Plato. I encountered it for the first time in its modern guise in 1970, the year when I embarked on a career in education, as a humanities teacher in a comprehensive school in Bristol, which coincided with the publication by Penguin of a series of radical books on education which unashamedly challenged teachers to embrace a critical pedagogy.

In today's educational climate – with its stress on 'delivery' and 'target-setting' – it is difficult to imagine an educational publisher issuing such a list. Most would judge that it wouldn't sell in sufficient numbers to achieve a profit, given the seemingly exceptionally high demand nowadays among teachers, especially those about to join the profession, for texts that eschew militant general ideas about schooling and education in favour of those that stress classroom tips, more often than not about behaviour-management. All too often, these books portray the classroom as a threatening environment inhabited by undermotivated and uninterested pupils, many of whom are assumed to be bent on causing difficulty. Rarely do they suggest that part of the problem of contemporary schooling might not be the pupils and their conduct, but rather the sort of curriculum to which they are subjected, which they often find boring, irrelevant and unrelated to their lives (Lodge 2003).

Unlike now, when the earlier Penguin series is largely ignored, in the more Romantically and idealistically disposed 1970s its titles were excitedly gobbled up by many radical teachers looking for ways of realizing practically the progressive educational outlooks to which they were committed. This explains why most of the Penguin texts went through a succession of reprints between 1970 and 1975 – as many as four in one case.

Certainly, when first issued, the books' titles articulated well with the kind of leftist pedagogical professional I then considered myself to be, and which in large and significant part I have remained. One was Everett Reimers' *School Is Dead*, which argued for alternatives in education; another was Paul Goodman's *Compulsory Miseducation*, which challenged the idea that education can only be achieved by having schools. But the volume which had the most impact on me at the time, and which was also the series' biggest seller, was Neil Postman's and Charles Weingartner's *Teaching as a Subversive Activity*.

Rereading this book now after a gap of many years reminds me of how extraordinarily progressive it was, and indeed remains. Written by two 'simple romantics' (which is how they describe themselves), it includes arguments that still, if only unconsciously, underpin and anticipate much current pedagogical theory, but which, sadly, do not influence policy for classroom practice.

Writing beyond what they describe as 'the constricting intimidation of conventional assumptions' (1971, p. 13), Postman and Weingartner say the following:

About the aims of education:
The new education has as its purpose the development of a new kind of person, one who ... is an actively, inquiring, flexible, creative, innovative, tolerant liberal personality who is able to face uncertainty and ambiguity without disorientation, who can formulate viable new meanings to meet changes in the environment which threaten individual and mutual survival.

(Postman and Weingartner, 1971, p. 204)

About the purpose of schooling:
We believe that schools must serve as the principal medium for

developing in youth the attitudes and skills of social, political and cultural criticism.

(p. 16)

About the 'good' teacher:
S/he believes that telling, when used as a basic teaching strategy, deprives students of the excitement of doing their own finding and of the opportunity for increasing their power as learners.

(p. 43)

S/he encourages student–student interaction as opposed to student–teacher interaction ... [S/he] is interested in students developing their own criteria or standards for judging the quality, precision and relevance of ideas. S/he permits such development to occur by minimizing her/his role as arbiter of what is acceptable and what is not.

(p. 44)

About 'teaching':
We have discovered in our attempts to install inquiry environments in various schools that great strides can be made if the words 'teach' and 'teaching' are simply subtracted from the operational lexicon.

(p. 47)

I am sure many teachers working in today's classrooms are happy to associate themselves with such statements, despite the fact that they rarely feature in official commentary about their work. Indeed, many such teachers successfully translate the underlying principles of Postman and Weingartner's progressive manifesto into imaginative learning opportunities for their pupils, frequently doing so in the guise of 'reflective practitioners' (Schon 1983), imbued with ideas from the 'teacher as researcher' tradition (Stenhouse 1975).

What is probably less the case is that they do so with the subversive intention of their predecessors, given the increasing extent of centralized prescription over what they can teach and the manner in which children's educational development, and by implication teachers' own practice, should be monitored and assessed. The result is that, while teachers no doubt retain and share a common desire to influence for the better, and in forward-looking ways, the educational progress of the children in their care, they are less inclined or encouraged than their counterparts were in the 1970s to be critical, independent thinkers.

It was easier to be such a teacher then of course, for the culture of the times allowed for it, and the absence of curtailing legislation offered a space in which it could happen. It is different now. Repressive central government policy for education has significantly domesticated and depoliticized many schoolteachers, not to mention their counterparts in universities and other centres of higher education, making them less likely than was the case 30 years ago to take on the function of 'organic intellectuals' (Gramsci 1971, pp. 3–24) within society, possessing the capacity to comment on and seek to influence aspects of public life.

But then intellectuals of all hues appear nowadays, especially in Britain, to live increasingly a life of cultural invisibility. Frank Furedi has caustically observed that today 'there do not appear to be very many prominent intellectual voices, and it is difficult to discern their collective impact on society'. Intellectuals, he argues, are 'an endangered species. In place of individuals possessing genuine learning, breadth of vision and a concern for public issues, we now have only facile pundits, think-tank apologists and spin doctors' (Furedi 2004, p. 26).

In my view, this assessment of Furedi's is both exaggerated and false. For while intellectualism as a universal function has never been a feature of any society, ancient or modern, it is simply untrue that British intellectuals today have become, or are just about to become, extinct. To be sure, the pull of glitzy celebrity culture, at one extreme, and the lure of increasing academic specialization, at the other, makes their impact less obvious than was maybe once the case (Collini 2006); but the idea that they have died out, or that there is now no room for them, is plain wrong, though it must be conceded that there prevails in British (compared, say, to mainland European) culture a degree of hostility to the idea of the intellectual – that is, of someone who, being well-read and highly informed, seeks to speak the truth intelligently about the big issues of contemporary public life, questioning often the established order of things. Indeed, in Britain, the label 'intellectual' is one that frequently triggers sneers, provoked by the suspicion that it points up an individual who is a too-clever-by-half poseur or, worse still, a person who takes condescending pleasure in claiming some kind of bookish superiority over lesser mortals.

When this does not happen, and when they are visible and active, such truth-speakers of course are not confined either to schools or universities or any centre of explicitly educational activity. Indeed, some make a virtue of not being linked to such places – for instance, left-wing radical Tariq Ali, the psychoanalyst Adam Phillips and the dramatist Harold Pinter. On the other hand, when intellectuals are located within the academy, they are more likely to be found in some academic departments than others. Thus it has been shown that disciplines generally identified as 'intellectual', including most of the humanities and social sciences, and education sometimes, typically produce more radicals than disciplines generally identified as natural-scientific or business and managerial; and that the greater the degree to which an individual within a given discipline identifies herself as an intellectual, the more likely s/he is to be a left-wing activist of one kind or another (Brym 1980). Additionally, despite the prominent cultural positions currently enjoyed by particular intellectuals, high status, within or without the academy, is not a defining characteristic of many of them, most forfeiting fame and fortune in favour of being free to fight for the truth as they see it. As such, intellectuals of this kind are defined less by position and more by a commitment to dialogue, argument and contrariness (Fuller 2005).

Such commitment has internal-psychological and external-sociological aspects. Internally, it frequently links with a disposition which enjoys revelling in the sheer bluster and cussedness of intellectual activity; externally, it always connects with at least one specific sociopolitical upheaval, or its prospect, giving rise to an extreme cultural reaction. In this chapter I want to illustrate how this process can work out in practice by discussing the kind of Romantic intellectualism personified in the radical attitude and declarations of William Hazlitt, showing how his robust and sometimes obdurate approach to criticism has important implications for how public educators might consider conducting themselves intellectually at the current juncture, which has its own peculiar upheavals. But, before I get to that, I need to do some scene-setting.

Journalism and Romanticism

In the course of placing the British Romantics within their historical setting, Marilyn Butler observes that several of them – Coleridge and Hazlitt in particular – thought it was their vocation to be professional intellectuals or 'men of letters', commenting upon events, personalities and associated trends during a period when the clamour for social reform was intense. Accordingly, Butler goes on to say, '[t]he search for Romanticism may be not so much the quest for a certain literary product, as for a type of producer' (Butler 1981, p. 70). The kind of intellectual producer brought forth by Romanticism, she correctly concludes, was significantly associated with the emergence in Britain in the late eighteenth and early nineteenth centuries of an astonishingly vibrant literary market in ideas, aided and abetted by the proliferation of high-quality books, newspapers, journals and magazines.

One of the most influential of these outlets was the radical *Edinburgh Review*, to which Hazlitt regularly contributed, and for which he was for a time a salaried reviewer. First published in 1802, this influential quarterly quickly established itself as one of the most significant cultural voices in Britain in the nineteenth century, reviewing everything worth knowing about in the fields of politics, society and the arts. Within ten years it was able to boast a circulation of well over 13,000, and an estimated readership of nearly four times that number (a great many subscribers and readers, even by today's standards). Its popularity among society's more bookish members, which was shared in significant part by other complementary periodicals, such as *The Examiner* and *The Political Register*, encouraged, in turn, the arrival on the cultural scene of the modern journalist 'not as a [mere] reporter ... but as [an intellectual] critic, watchdog and self-appointed spokesman for the individual citizen' (Butler 1981, p. 70). Several of the Romantic writers who feature in this book took on this role with enthusiasm. Wordsworth, for example, alongside his activities as a poet, wrote political pamphlets; while Coleridge published a considerable amount of political and social commentary. But it was Hazlitt who embraced this function more than any other British Romantic, publishing in his short life a mass of critical essays and reviews which together amount to a profound and radical intellectual oeuvre. But what kind of critic was he? And what can we learn from his style of criticism?

Hazlitt's intellectualism

Hazlitt possessed a 'non-signing-up' kind of mind, a mode of critical intelligence to which we can gain insight from reading parts of his (1819) essay 'Lectures on the English Comic Writers', where he says this about the sixteenth-century French essayist Michel de Montaigne:

> The great merit of Montaigne ... was that he may be said to have been the first who had the courage to say as an author what he felt as a man ... He was, in the truest sense, a man of original mind – that is, he had the power of looking at things for himself, or as they really were, instead of blindly trusting to, and fondly repeating what others told him that they were ... In taking up his pen he did not set up for a philosopher, wit, orator, or moralist, but he became all of these by merely daring to tell us whatever passed through his mind, in its naked simplicity and force ...

He did not ... undertake to say all that can be said upon a subject, but what, in his capacity as an inquirer after truth, he happened to know about. He was neither a pedant nor a bigot. He neither supposed that he was bound to know all things, nor that all things were bound to conform to what he had fancied or would have them to be. In treating of men and manners, he spoke of them as he found them, not according to preconceived notions and abstract dogmas; and he began by teaching us what he himself was ... He was, in a word, the first author who was not a book-maker, and who wrote not to make converts of others ... but to satisfy his own mind of the truth of things.

(Wu 1998, Vol. 5, p. 85)

Hazlitt could be writing here as much about himself as about Montaigne. For, like his hero, Hazlitt had an original mind, refusing always to repeat 'what others told him', without first subjecting this to questioning. And, like Montaigne, he wrote and spoke about things as 'he found them', never relying on 'preconceived notions and abstract dogmas', except that of justice, the nature of which he derived not from membership of any political party or movement – studiously avoiding such things, being independent of everything other than his own intellect – but, typically, from his appreciation of literature, and Shakespeare in particular. Here (in his 'Characters of Shakespeare's Plays', which appeared in 1815) Hazlitt writes about *Coriolanus*, a drama concerning an arrogant, obstinate autocrat that loathes the common people, who return his hate:

Shakespeare has in this play shewn himself well versed in history and state affairs. *Coriolanus* is a store-house of political common-places ... The arguments for and against aristocracy or democracy, on the privileges of the few and the claims of the many, on liberty and slavery, power and the abuse of it, peace and war, are here very ably handled, with the spirit of a poet and the acuteness of a philosopher ...

(Wu 1998, Vol. 1, p. 125)

While loathing Coriolanus's abuse of state power, Hazlitt is equally contemptuous of those who are cowardly and submit to it:

The tame submission to usurped authority ... has nothing to excite or flatter the imagination ... The love of power in ourselves and the admiration of it in others are both natural to man: the one makes him a tyrant, the other a slave ... The whole dramatic moral of *Coriolanus* is that those who have little shall have less, and those who have much

shall take all that others have left ... [W]hat is sport to the few is death
to the many.

(Wu 1998, Vol. 1, p. 126)

On the other hand, in hating far more the corruption, hypocrisy and
apostasy of society's 'betters', Hazlitt is best recalled politically and
intellectually as a secular republican who consistently raged against the
way in which powerful minorities, monarchs in particular, sought to
subjugate majorities, limiting their freedom of expression and livelihood. To
that extent, he was always a fully paid-up member of the non-existent Party
of Justice and Democracy, making him in many ways like that contemporary
man of letters the late Edward Said, who once defined the intellectual (and
by implication himself) as a person 'set apart, someone who is able to speak
the truth to power, a crusty, eloquent, fantastically courageous and angry
individual for whom no worldly power is too big and imposing to be
criticized and pointedly taken to task' (Said 1994, p. 7) and, elsewhere, as 'an
opponent of consensus and orthodoxy', acting as 'a kind of public memory; to
recall what is forgotten or ignored; to connect and contextualize and to
generalize from what appear to be the fixed truths' (Said 2001a, pp. 502–3).

Like Hazlitt, Said was, as a recent editor puts it, 'always at a slight
tangent to his affinities' (Judt 2004, p. ix). Indeed, Hazlitt's and Said's
stubborn refusal to be categorized and captured by any particular
factional interest made them both outsiders, standing 'between loneliness
and alignment' (Said 1994, p. 17). It also led to acrimonious conflict with
their peers, generating awkward public disputation. The well-known
intemperate exchanges between Edward Said and Ernest Gellner on the
'orientalist question' (see Irwin 2007), which featured in the reviews and
letters pages of the *Times Literary Supplement* in February 1993, for example,
have an historical parallel in those which contributed finally to a severance
of relations between Hazlitt and Coleridge. A brief recounting of the
circumstances surrounding the latter case is instructive at this point
because they highlight a further important aspect of the intellectual's role
– principled steadfastness, exercised without fear of personal consequences.

Hazlitt versus Coleridge

The high estimation in which Hazlitt initially held Coleridge is the stuff of
literary legend, having its origins in an extraordinary first encounter
involving the two men on Sunday 14 January 1798 in Shrewsbury's
Unitarian church, to which the latter had been invited to deliver an

oration. Hazlitt was in the congregation. Along with everyone else present, he listened with rapt attention to what Coleridge had to say, recalling affectionately his impressions of the occasion in that most brilliant of his essays, 'On My First Acquaintance with Poets', published many years afterwards in 1823 (see also Holmes 1999b, pp. 178–81 and Grayling 2000, pp. 51–7).

Hazlitt, with no reputation whatsoever, was just 18 at the time; Coleridge, who was already showing promise as a revolutionary lecturer, poet and journalist, was 26. Coleridge's sermon, Hazlitt tells us, was brilliantly paced, eloquently delivered and richly illustrated: 'I could not have been more delighted if I had heard the music of the spheres. Poetry and Philosophy had met together. Truth and genius had embraced ... I returned home well satisfied' (Wu 1998, 9, p. 97). But that was not the end of it, for Hazlitt encountered Coleridge at his father's house just two days later, where, over dinner, he was mesmerized by the visitor's erudition and intelligence. Accompanying Coleridge on the walk from his home back to Shrewsbury, Hazlitt was further stunned by Coleridge's lucidity: 'In digressing, in dilating, in passing from subject to subject, he appeared to me to float in air, to slide on ice' (Wu 1998, 9, p. 100). Coleridge also took an interest in Hazlitt's ideas, which both flattered and encouraged him in equal measure. Their relationship was thus well begun, and its importance to Hazlitt cannot be underestimated. He admired the older man immensely, which makes their later collision and eventual separation tragic but perhaps inevitable, given Hazlitt's loathing of intellectual inconsistency and moral and political hypocrisy, of which he eventually believed Coleridge to be guilty.

All of this was brought to its anguished denouement by the political and social events in England leading up to the suspension of Habeas Corpus in March 1817. For 20 or more years previously, England's civil and political societies had been seriously at odds with each other – appalling levels of poverty afflicted large sections of the urban and rural working class, and the nation's electoral system was shockingly inconsistent and discriminatory – giving rise to an avalanche of demands for parliamentary and social reform from radical groups and individuals. The increasing stridency of these appeals aroused great anxiety among the ruling class of the time, who feared a revolution unless measures were taken, not to meet the demands of the reform movement, but to frustrate and curtail the activities of its advocates. Progressive journalists such as Hazlitt were singled out as particularly dangerous and seditious enemies of the state.

The government came down hard: it took control of reading-rooms in a move to block circulation of radical literature and sought to curtail the right to meet and protest, harassing individuals whom it judged organizers of dissent. In the Spa Fields meeting of December 1816, the ring-leaders were arrested and charged with treason, and John Cashman, an individual protester, was successfully tried for looting and sedition, for which he received the death penalty, brutally carried out in public in front of an angry mob in central London three months later (see Paulin 1998, pp. 175–6). Three years later a similar meeting at St Peter's Field, Manchester, resulted in the troops being called out. Eleven civilians were cut down and killed; hundreds were wounded.

These, then, were extraordinary times, and Hazlitt was never cautious for his own safety in making his voice heard about them, particularly in his voluminous *Political Essays*. Coleridge, meanwhile, whom one might have expected to side with the protesters and to ally himself with the likes of Hazlitt, publicly sat on his hands as events unfolded. Privately, however, he lent support to the government's repressive acts. Thus, in a confidential letter sent by him to the then prime minister, Lord Liverpool, dated 28 July 1817 – despatched four months after the suspension of Habeas Corpus and the execution of John Cashman – Coleridge, in addition to pledging absolute loyalty to the state, invites God, no less, to grant 'that under the wise and temperate measures of [his] Lordship, the necessary process may be carried on in meekness and by individual collisions'.

Hazlitt did not know of this letter. If he had, one can only guess at the level his denunciation of Coleridge's faithlessness might have reached. Instead, he indirectly attacked Coleridge's failure to engage publicly with the political realities of the day through a series of coruscating critical reviews of poetic and other works of his which appeared at about the same time. So, in September 1816, in *The Examiner*, Hazlitt condemns Coleridge's authorship of *The Statesman's Manual*: 'All that he does or thinks is involuntary; even his perversity and self-will are so. They are nothing but a necessity of yielding to the slightest motive. Everlasting inconsequentiality marks all he does.' Then in November 1816, in the *Edinburgh Review*, Hazlitt censures Coleridge's recently published *Christabel*, declaring it to be 'utterly destitute of value, [exhibiting] not a ray of genius ... [T]here is literally not one couplet in the publication ... which would be reckoned poetry, or even sense, were it found in the corner of a newspaper or upon the window of an inn.' The following year, Hazlitt assaults Coleridge still further, again in the *Edinburgh Review*, writing:

Mr Coleridge [flies], not in the air, but underground – playing at hawk and buzzard between sense and nonsense, – floating or sinking in fine Kantean categories, in a state of suspended animation 'twixt dreaming and awake, – quitting the plain ground of 'history and particular facts' for the first butterfly theory, fancy-bred from the maggots of his brain – going up in an air-balloon filled with fetid gas. (All quotations are derived from Wu 2006).

Hazlitt, then, was appalled by Coleridge's perfidy, mealy-mouthedness and obtuse abstractionism, and all the more so because of his previous deep admiration of the poet-philosopher's genius and radicalism, both of which he considered to have been frittered away over the intervening years, while he, meanwhile, remained constant, continuing to speak the truth to power as a spokesman for society's exploited and less articulate members. Hazlitt's irritation was also motivated by the knowledge that, unlike himself, because of Coleridge's status as a public figure, he was well placed to at least attempt to exercise some progressive influence over the course of political events as they were being orchestrated by the government of the day. Instead, we learn that, behind the scenes, Coleridge was doing the exact opposite, toadying up to political power rather than challenging it. As Grayling says: '[Hazlitt] was incensed by hypocrisy and apostasy; he could not forgive a man [like Coleridge] who had [previously] ... vocally sympathized with the plight of mankind, but [who] then turned away to feather his own nest by fawning on the powers that created that plight' (Grayling 2000, p. 217).

The challenge of self-consistency

None of this, despite appearances to the contrary, came easily to Hazlitt, who found the condition of self-consistency sometimes very hard going, acknowledging on more than one occasion the fatal pull and irreversible finality of going against one's long-held political opinions:

It requires an effort of resolution, or at least obstinate prejudice, for a man to maintain his opinions at the expense of his interest. But it requires a much greater effort of resolution for a man to give up his interest to recover his independence ... A man, in adhering to his principles in contradiction to the decisions of the world, has disadvantages. He has nothing to support him but the supposed sense of right; and any defect in the justice of his cause, or the force of his conviction, must prey on his mind, in proportion to the delicacy and sensitiveness of its texture; he is left alone in his opinions; and ... grows nervous, melancholy, fantastical, and would be glad of somebody or anybody to sympathize with him ...

(Wu 1998, 4, p. 129)

Hazlitt understood fully what this process required of him, and by inference and projection we can discern what it means for anyone today seeking to be an intellectual. 'Nothing [he writes] but the strongest and clearest conviction can support a man in a losing minority' (Grayling 2000, p. 217). The implication of this message for today's intellectuals, educational and otherwise, is not difficult to spell out. At a minimum, it requires them to review periodically the degree to which they are able to retain an appropriate critical distance from government and other forms of authority, avoiding pressures to become incorporated into their political and social agendas. Education academics, on this understanding, might choose to be a 'critical friend' of state power, but never at the expense of their independent judgement, which at times might lead them to oppose the policies of particular Education Secretaries. That is the risk and the responsibility of criticism, which requires moral courage and persistency, akin to the qualities identified earlier in Chapter 5 in my discussion of heroism in teaching, learning and leading.

The intellectual essay

Although such opposition needs continuously to seek out new ways to express itself and exert influence, there remains one means of communication that arguably retains, since Hazlitt's day, the power to persuade and encourage. I am referring here to the literary essay, which constitutes a highly accessible and personal way of writing that has the effect both of liberating the worldliness of intellectuals who use it, and of facilitating big and positive impacts on their readers as a result.

Education academics do not much use this literary form to communicate their ideas, short newspaper articles excepted. Only rarely, for example, do they utilize significant outlets for the publication of extended essays to disseminate their critical analyses. I cannot recall, for example, last reading an education-specific essay in *The London Review of Books*, though the April 2006 edition of *Prospect* featured Alison Wolff's provocative discussion of the social consequences of women's higher education and Robert Jackson's commentary on the future of higher education. More typically, education academics, make use of professional high-status journals to make their views known. This is sad, chiefly because much of what they choose to say in them is inaccessible to other intellectuals who do not function in the field of education and with whom, presumably, they might wish to make contact.

The literary essay circumvents this limitation, chiefly through its immediacy, which encourages its users, in Said's words, 'to become thoroughly implicated in their revulsions' (2001c, p. 30). Elsewhere, Said compares essay-writing with piano-playing: 'The essay, like the recital, is occasional, re-creative, and personal' (2001b, p. 229). In similar vein, Tom Paulin conceives of the essay as one means 'to combine the advantages of the literary and the conversational styles', as something that is 'random, chancy, sparky'; a printed text 'that aspires to the condition of rapid, direct, inspired speech'; a kind of 'improvised one-act play taking place in a writer's studio' (1998, pp. 271ff.). To that extent, after William Burroughs, it is a form of writing that aspires 'to make things happen' (1985, p. 61) – action in prose form, in other words.

Paulin observes that the critical act for Hazlitt, 'expressed in a vigorous, flexible, fast-moving prose style', is 'analogous to the creative process by which [he and] every mind knows and understands' (Paulin 1998, pp. 24– 5). This, he maintains, gives rise to a distinctive voice and literary style – a form of prose akin to kinetic performance. Hazlitt's, Paulin says, is a muscular, sinewy, active, gymnastic, declamatory form of writing – a confident, heroic and direct way of communicating that 'sings in its reach and stretch' (Paulin 1998, p. 22). Quickfire, intense, often pictorial, Hazlitt's writings embody 'buzz, activity, gusto, as against fixed concepts' (op cit., p. 33). Indeed, in his own final collection of essays, *The Plain Speaker*, Hazlitt likens his preferred literary style to extempore speaking and the painting of frescos, 'which imply a life of study and great previous preparation, but of which the execution is momentary and irrevocable'.

The Plain Speaker, in fact, signals directly the presence of the spoken word in Hazlitt's writing. As Paulin remarks, his intention in this volume is to convey the idea of immediacy in written communication as a powerful physical sensation in which 'every word should be a blow, every hit should tell' (Paulin 1998, p. 284). Bold honesty; boisterous, unbuttoned plain speaking; turbulent risk-taking; free rational enquiry; communication; liberty; democracy – these themes reverberate through Hazlitt's discourse in *The Plain Speaker*, in which he realizes a prose that 'positions itself confidently, glowing with chipper good health' (Paulin 1998, p. 292). Here is an example of it, taken from one of the best-known of the essays in *The Plain Speaker* – 'On the Prose-Style of Poets' – in which Hazlitt comments admiringly on the writing style of one of his heroes, the parliamentarian Edmund Burke:

> It has always appeared to me that the most prefect prose style, the most powerful, the most dazzling, the most daring, that which went the nearest to the verge of poetry, and yet never fell over, was Burke's . . . Its

style is airy, flighty, adventurous, but it never loses sight of the subject; nay, is always in contact with, and derives its increased or varying impulse from it ... It differs from poetry, as I conceive, like the chamois from the eagle: it climbs to an almost equal height, touches upon a cloud, overlooks a precipice, is picturesque, sublime – but all the while, instead of soaring through the air, it stands upon a rocky cliff, clambers up by abrupt and intricate ways, and browses on the roughest bark, or crops the tender flower. The principle that guides his pen is truth, not beauty – not pleasure, but power.

(Wu 1998, 8, pp. 7–8)

It is not my intention to commend unqualifiedly to education academics and other critics the form of prose writing developed and advocated by Hazlitt, least of all the kind I have just illustrated. In any event, it is not child's play to write like Hazlitt, as he himself once admitted: 'It is not easy to write a familiar style. Many people mistake a familiar style for a vulgar style, and suppose that to write without affectation is to write at random. On the contrary, there is nothing that requires more precision, and, if I may say so, purity of expression, than the style I am speaking of' (Wu 1998, 6, p. 217).

However, what I am suggesting is that educationists should adopt a bolder and more combative style when writing about their vision for the future of education. And why? Because the dry-as-dust stuff they too often write and publish now rarely inspires readers and fellow professionals to think differently and imaginatively about the possibility of school reform and of the role they might play in bringing it about. This may partly explain why the Penguin series I mentioned at the start of this chapter proved so popular when first issued, for many of its books were vividly and inspirationally written.

Critical lessons from Hazlitt

Hazlitt teaches us that a passion for the truth is crucial for the intellectual life. He also indicates that, in making oneself heard and understood as an intellectual, it may be necessary from time to time to use forms of writing that eschew academic abstractionism in favour of a more passionate style. To appreciate this last point, there is no substitute for reading Hazlitt (rather than my or anybody else's commentary on what he wrote). And that is quite an experience, whatever one thinks of his subject matter and point of view about it. Indeed, as one of his admirers remarks, 'no one can read him without responding to the vigour of his thought and style, for he wrote with a steady, throbbing power that seems to generate a torrent of ideas' (Baker 1962, pp. 469–70). This is true, and the reason for this is provided by Hazlitt himself via his description of the art of an anonymous critic, in that most famous of his essays, from which I also quoted a moment ago, 'On the Prose-Style of Poets':

> The principle which guides his pen is truth, not beauty – not pleasure, but power. He has no choice, no selection of subject to flatter the reader's idle taste, or assist his own fancy: he must take what comes, and make the most of it. He works the most striking effects out of the most uncompromising materials, by the mere activity of his mind ... In prose, the professed object is to impart conviction, and nothing can be admitted by way of ornament or relief, that does not add new force or to clearness to the original conception ... There must be a weight, a precision, a conformity from association in the tropes and figures of animated prose to fit them to their place in the argument, and make them tell.
>
> (Wu 1998, Vol. 8, pp. 7–8)

Hazlitt's conception here of criticism as an act of persuasive eloquence is maybe one that today is difficult to emulate in the education context where teachers and lecturers are constrained by targets and audits and by a market in educational knowledge that often requires them to kowtow to authority. On the other hand, it may serve to remind many of us who work in education of our vocation to be public intellectuals as well as pedagogues – indeed, to regard the former as instantiated in the latter, requiring us to be constant, rigorous and unapologetic in facing down falsehood and the corruption of ideas generally.

Conclusion

A serious intellectual discussion is never characterized by a definitive ending, but rather by a temporary settlement of, or impermanent retreat from, the issues with which it deals, holding out the prospect of resuming conversation about them when need and opportunity arises, notably as new ideas and evidence become available which call out to be tested dialogically.

This 'conclusion' is thus not designed to express my final word about the concerns identified and discussed in the course of this book.. How could it be otherwise? For mine has been both an extremely partial and highly selective account of the Romantic underpinnings of progressive education – one which consequently lays itself wide open to criticism, outright rejection even. Indeed, because this book is written to disrupt, I should not be surprised – and won't be – when it evokes (as it is bound to) hostile reaction from educators who do not share either my pedagogical outlook or my philosophy of education. There will also be those more sympathetic readers who will object that I haven't said enough about this or that aspect, with others drawing attention to things I ought to have discussed, but didn't. I am at ease about such criticism, taking my lead from the eminent philosopher of science Karl Popper, who, when replying to his many critics on one occasion, remarked that 'it is not possible to say, at the same time, all that can be said about any topic' (Schlipp 1974, p. 1167).

So what am I doing here, then, if I am not concluding? The answer is that I am not so much producing an ending as signalling a wish merely to stop for a while – to take stock and, most importantly, to begin to anticipate what my readers make of it all, knowing that further good conversation about Romance and education awaits me if I listen carefully to what they have to say. Stopping and taking stock, on the other hand, legitimates my wish to write a brief coda – specifically, an additional passage in which I briefly outline some after-the-event thoughts of my own about the journey I anticipated making in the Preface, and from which I now want to take a short break.

These thoughts centre on two matters. The first is to do with a recent
event in public life in the UK, the focus of which reassures me that the sort
of arguments I have outlined in this book are at least worth having, even if
my engagement with them here is seen as inadequate; the second is to do
with the Romantic vision itself and the possibility of its realization in the
education context and ones like it. The first matter is about relevance and
confidence; the second is about realism and optimism.

The event was the publication in the *Daily Telegraph* on 12 September
2006 of a letter, co-signed by 110 teachers, psychologists, academics,
authors, children's experts and early-years specialists, calling on the
government to act 'to prevent the death of childhood'.

It read as follows:

As professionals and academics from a range of backgrounds, we are
deeply concerned at the escalating incidence of childhood depression
and children's behavioural and developmental conditions. We believe
this is largely due to a lack of understanding, on the part of both
politicians and the general public, of the realities and subtleties of child
development.

Since children's brains are still developing, they cannot adjust – as
full-grown adults can – to the effects of ever more rapid technological
and cultural change. They still need what developing human beings
have always needed, including real food (as opposed to processed
'junk'), real play (as opposed to sedentary, screen-based entertain-
ment), first-hand experience of the world they live in and regular
interaction with the real-life significant adults in their lives.

They also need time. In a fast-moving hyper-competitive culture,
today's children are expected to cope with an ever-earlier start to
formal schoolwork and an overly academic test-driven primary
curriculum. They are pushed by market forces to act and dress like
mini-adults and exposed via the electronic media to material which
would have been considered unsuitable for children even in the very
recent past.

Our society rightly takes great pains to protect children from physical
harm, but seems to have lost sight of their emotional and social needs.
However, it's now clear that the mental health of an unacceptable
number of children is being unnecessarily compromised, and that this is
almost certainly a key factor in the rise of substance abuse, violence and
self-harm amongst our young people.

This is a complex socio-cultural problem to which there is no simple
solution, but a sensible first step would be to encourage parents and

policy-makers to start talking about ways of improving children's well-being. We therefore propose as a matter of urgency that public debate be initiated on child-rearing in the 21st century. This issue should be central to public policy-making in coming decades.

On the day of the letter's publication, one of its signatories, the children's author Jacqueline Wilson, was reported to have said:

> We are not valuing childhood. I speak to children at book-signings and they ask me how I go through the process of writing and I say, 'Oh, you know, it's just like when you play imaginary games and you simply write it all down.' All I get back are blank faces. I don't think some children use their imaginations anymore. (Quoted in Fenton 2006, p. 1)

The letter brought in its wake a huge public response, most of it sympathetic and supportive, though there was some cautionary and a little oppositional reaction. Ed Mayo of the UK National Consumer Council, for example, writing in the *Guardian*, (16 Sept 2006), while welcoming the experts' intervention, made a special plea for children's needs to be listened and responded to as they, rather than adult society, define them. Similarly, Agnes Nairn, a researcher from Bath, argued that discussions about childhood in contemporary society need to include children themselves, most of whom are too often left out of the deliberative process by adults anxious about their welfare: 'This is not to say they don't need our help to navigate their way through. But why don't we work through the issues with the children and include them in the debate?' Anne Karpf (*Guardian* 21 Sept 2006), echoing this sentiment, urged that the discussion be extended to take in the welfare of adults too, since 'late capitalism is bad for [everyone's] mental health – whatever age you are' (2006, p. 13).

But these mildly critical reactions to the original letter did not render its appeal and importance any less significant.[1] No one seriously opposed the idea of having a debate about childhood, although some scornful liberals appeared reluctant to admit the possibility that any aspect of life in the past might be preferable to existence today. Fearing that if they agreed to be party to such a debate they would be branded as conservative or – worse still – as unsophisticated 'golden-ageists', such liberals slid out of view and contention. Well, not entirely, for one of them, in the course of being interviewed on the radio following the letter's publication, felt compelled to abuse the initiative, remarking that 'what we don't want is to recreate a romantic idea of childhood'.

While the irony of this comment was completely lost on its interlocutor, I am hoping that it might not be on readers of this book. For the conception of childhood which my Romantics of choice first brought into existence – and which I discussed at length in Chapter 2 – is an extremely progressive one from which today we might relearn many things. Certainly, Blake and Wordsworth emphasize the huge potential of childhood, drawing attention to the importance of viewing it as a glorious period in its own right, rather than as one that acts merely as a preparation for adulthood. In addition, all the Romantics (as I made clear in Chapter 6) held sophisticated views about the imaginative life – about its nature, importance and necessity. To that extent, their contribution is as relevant to our times, including the issues raised by that *Daily Telegraph* letter, as it was to theirs, giving us not only a rich source of ideas to help combat contemporary forms of unimaginativeness, as these impact on children and adults alike, but also the confidence to do so knowing that our arguments have a long and distinguished pedigree.

But being on the right side of an argument does not make what it is about any the more realizable. This was brought home to me in the course of presenting some of the ideas in Chapter 4 on 'loving pedagogy' at a seminar last year. One of those present – a primary schoolteacher, who was very tired from a day's teaching – said to me: 'OK, I agree with you, but only in theory, because all day today I have been trying to teach children, some of whom, quite frankly, were unlovable. And you ask me to love them! How is this possible?' The answer is that it isn't always. Sometimes one has to settle, for the moment, or for the time being, for second best. It isn't possible continuously to act virtuously as a teacher at the highest possible level. Backsliding is a chronic feature of the moral life, whether played out in the classroom or beyond it. The crucial thing, it seems to me, is to hold on to the *possibility* of being a Romantic progressive educator – to have it as an ideal tucked away, so to speak, in one's metaphorical pocket, to be retrieved and to think and act better with as circumstances allow. This is not a fanciful suggestion. For, as I have said more than once in this book, many teachers are Romantics without really knowing it. Realizing this fact in critically conscious ways, I have also argued from the outset, is one means of helping them to rekindle or reinforce a pedagogy that is genuinely educational because it is explicitly progressive.

There is nothing inevitable about any of this, of course. But it is unlikely to happen without some educational vision to which to aspire or some notion of the Good in teaching and learning against which to evaluate one's practice as a teacher. My argument has been that Romanticism – as a mood, a set of ideas and an attitude – offers an optimistic and realistic prospectus for teachers anxious to do just that. It also acts to remind education's public intellectuals of their duty to maintain hope on behalf of the rest of us.

I am reminded finally of Wordsworth's claim that teaching is an inescapable aspect of being a poet. His view that the creative capacity of poets enables them to have singular insight into the ways of the world led him to believe they had a special pedagogical responsibility to communicate this knowledge to less imaginative, unpoetic individuals who did not. As public educators, few of us are, like Wordsworth, great poet-teachers. On the other hand, following his lead, and that of his fellow Romantics, we can at least aspire, in our educational work, to be one in our hearts, minds and actions, embracing Romantic love, heroism, criticism and the life of the imagination as we do so.

Note

1 On the contrary, a UNICEF Report published a few months afterwards (*An Overview of Child Well-Being in Rich Countries*) draws graphic attention to the risks and insecurities suffered by many children in the UK and elsewhere in the world.

References

Adams, T.T. (2004) 'Heroes and villains', *Observer Magazine*, 19 December.

Albrecht, W.P (1965) *Hazlitt and the Creative Imagination*, Lawrence, KA: University of Kansas.

Armstrong, J. (2003) *Conditions of Love: The Philosophy of Intimacy*, London: Penguin.

Armstrong, L. (2001) *It's Not about the Bike: My Journey Back to Life*, London: Yellow Jersey Press.

Atkinson, T. and Claxton, G. (2000) (eds) *The Intuitive Practitioner*, Buckingham: Open University Press.

Badhwar, N.K. (2005) 'Love', in H. La Follette (ed.), *The Oxford Handbook of Practical Ethics*, Oxford: Oxford University Press.

Baker, H. (1962) *William Hazlitt*, Oxford: Oxford University Press.

Barker, J. (2000) *Wordsworth: A Life*, London: Penguin.

Barrow, R. (1988) 'Some observations on the concept of imagination', in Egan and Nadaner 1988.

Bate, W.J. (1961) *From Classic to Romantic: Premises of Taste in Eighteenth-Century England*, New York: Harper.

—— (2003) *John Clare: A Biography*, London: Picador.

Bauman, Z. (2003) *Liquid Love: On the Frailty of Human Bonds*, Cambridge: Polity Press.

—— (2005) *Liquid Life*, Cambridge: Polity Press.

Beck, U. and Beck-Gernsheim, E. (1995) *The Normal Chaos of Love*, Cambridge: Polity Press.

Berlin, I. (1999) *The Roots of Romanticism*, Princeton, NJ: Princeton University Press.

Bernstein, B. (2000) *Pedagogy, Symbolic Control and Identity*, Lantham, MD: Rowman & Littlefield.

Blades, J. (2004) *Wordsworth and Coleridge: Lyrical Ballads*, Basingstoke: Palgrave-Macmillan.

Bloom, H. (1986) (ed.) *William Hazlitt*, New York: Chelsea.

Blythe, R. (1970) Introduction. In W. Hazlitt, *Selected Writings*, London: Penguin.

Bowra, C.M. (1961) *The Romantic Imagination*, Oxford: Oxford University Press.

Bromwich, D. (1999) *Hazlitt: The Mind of a Critic*, New Haven, CT: Yale University Press.

Bronowski, (ed.) (1958) *William Blake: A Selection of Poems and Letters*, Harmondsworth: Penguin.

Brookner, A. (2001) *Romanticism and its Discontents*, London: Penguin.

Brym, R. J. (1980) *Intellectuals and Politics*, London: George Allen & Unwin.

Buber, M. (1946) *Between Man and Man*, London: Kegan Paul.

Burroughs, W. (1985) *The Adding Machine*, London: Calder.

Butler, M. (1981) *Romantics, Rebels and Reactionaries: English Literature and its Background 1760–1830*, Oxford: Oxford University Press.

Caldwell, B.J. and Spinks, J.M. (1992) *Leading the Self-Managing School*, London: Falmer.

Campbell, C. (1989) *The Romantic Ethic and the Spirit of Modern Consumerism*, Oxford: Basil Blackwell.

Cho, D. (2005) 'Lessons of love; psychoanalysis and teacher–student love', *Educational Theory*, 55.1: 79–92.

Clarke, F. (1940) *Education and Social Change: An English Interpretation*, London: Sheldon Press.

Collini, S. (2006) *Absent Minds: Intellectuals in Britain*, Oxford: Oxford University Press.

Comte-Sponville, A. (2003) *A Short Treatise on the Great Virtues*, London: Vintage.

Connell, P. (2001) *Romanticism, Economics and the Question of Culture*, Oxford: Oxford University Press.

Cook, J. (2007) *Hazlitt in Love: a fatal attraction*, London: Short Books.

Cunningham, H. (1991) *The Children of the Poor: Representations of Childhood since the Seventeenth Century*, Oxford: Basil Blackwell.

— (1995) *Children and Childhood in Western Society since 1500*, Harlow: Longman.

Day, A. (1996) *Romanticism*, London: Routledge.

Day, C. (2004) *A Passion for Teaching*, London: RoutledgeFalmer.

Dearden, R.F. (1968) *The Philosophy of Primary Education*, London: Routledge & Kegan Paul.

—— (1972) 'Happiness and education', in R.F. Dearden, P.H. Hirst and R.S. Peters (eds), *Education and the Development of Reason*, London: Routledge & Kegan Paul.

Dixon, J. (1999) *The Romance Fiction of Mills and Boon 1909–1990*, London: UCL Press.

Duff, D. (1998) 'From revolution to romanticism: the historical context', in D. Wu (ed.), *A Companion to Romanticism*, Oxford: Blackwell.

Egan, K. (1990) *Romantic Understanding: The Development of Rationality and Imagination, Ages 8–15*, London: Routledge.

—— (1992) *Imagination in Teaching and Learning*, London: Routledge.

Egan, K. and Nadaner, D. (eds) (1988) Introduction, *Imagination and Education*, Milton Keynes: Open University Press.

Eisner, E.W. (1979) *The Educational Imagination*, New York: Macmillan.

Elliott, R.K. (1974) 'Education, love of subject, love of truth', *Proceedings of the Philosophy of Education Society of Great Britain*, 8.1: 135–53.

Epstein, J. (1991) 'Hazlitt's passions, The New Criterion', www.newcriterion. com/archive/10/nov91/hazlitt.htm

Fenton, B. (2006) 'Junk culture is poisoning our children', *Daily Telegraph*, 12 September, p. 1.

Fisher, M. (1990) *Personal Love*, London: Duckworth.

Foot, M. (1986) 'The Shakespeare prose writer', in Bloom (ed.) 1986.

Foucault, M. (1977) *Discipline and Punish: The Birth of the Prison*, London: Allen Lane.

Fried, R. (1995) *The Passionate Teacher*, Boston, MA: Beacon Press.

Friedenberg, E.Z. (1990) 'Romanticism and alternatives to schooling', in Willensky (ed.) 1990.

Fuchs, B. (2004) *Romance*, London: Routledge.

Fulford, T. (1999) *Romanticism and Masculinity*, New York: Macmillan.

Fuller, S. (2005) *The Intellectual*, London: Icon Books.

Furedi, F. (2004) *Where Have All the Intellectuals Gone?*, London: Continuum.

Garrison, J. (1997) *Dewey and Eros: Wisdom and Desire in the Art of Teaching*, New York: Teachers College.

Giddens, A. (1992) *The Transformation of Intimacy: Sexuality, Love and Eroticism in Modern Societies*, Cambridge: Polity Press.

Gill, S. (1984) *William Wordsworth: A Critical Edition of the Major Works*, Oxford: Oxford University Press.

—— (1989) *William Wordsworth: A Life*, Oxford: Clarendon Press.

Goldstein, L.S. (2004) 'Loving teacher education', in Liston and Garrison (eds) 2004.

Gosden, P.H.J.H. (1969) *How They Were Taught*, Oxford: Basil Blackwell.

Gramsci, A. (1971) *Selections from the Prison Notebooks of Antonio Gramsci*, London: Lawrence & Wishart.

Grayling, A.C. (2000) *The Quarrel of the Age: The Life and Times of William Hazlitt*, London: Weidenfeld & Nicolson.

Grice, D. (2004) 'Optimism grows as MacArthur hits the sack', *Guardian*, 15 December, p. 22.

Halpin, D. (2003) *Hope and Education: The Role of the Utopian Imagination*, London: Routledge.

Halpin, D. and Moore, A. (2000) 'Maintaining, reconstructing and creating tradition in education', *Oxford Review of Education*, 26.2: 133–44.

Heath, D. and Boreham, J. (1999) *Introducing Romanticism*, Cambridge: Icon Books.

Heffernan, J.A.W. (1969) *Wordsworth's Theory of Poetry: The Transforming Imagination*, Ithaca, NY: Cornell University Press.

Hirst, P.H. (1973) 'What is teaching?' In R.S. Peters (ed.), *The Philosophy of Education*, Oxford: Oxford University Press.

Hofkosh, S. (1998) *Sexual Politics and the Romantic Author*, Cambridge: Cambridge University Press.

Hogan, P. (1996) 'Forlorn hopes and great expectations: teaching as a way of life in an age of uncertainty', *Irish Educational Studies*, 16: 1–18.

Holmes, R. (1999a) *Coleridge: Early Visions*, London: Flamingo.

—— (1999b) *Coleridge: Darker Reflections*, London: Flamingo.

Hopps, D.D. (2004) 'MacArthur wins battle to keep challenge alive', *Guardian*, 14 December.

Howe, P.P. (1928–32) *The Complete Works of William Hazlitt* (21 volumes), London: J.M. Dent & Sons.

Hughes-Hallett, L. (2004) *Heroes, Saviours, Traitors and Supermen*, London: Fourth Estate.

Humphries, M. and Hyland, T. (2002) 'Theory, practice and performance in teaching: professionalism, intuition and jazz', *Educational Studies*, 28.1: 5–15.

Irwin, R. (2007) *For Lust of Knowing: The Orientalists and their Enemies*, London: Penguin.

Jackson, P.W. (1968) *Life in Classrooms*, New York: Holt, Rinehart & Winston.

James, A., Jenks, C. and Prout, A. (1998) *Theorizing Childhood*, Cambridge: Polity Press.

Jenks, C. (1996) *Childhood*, London: Routledge.

Jimack, P.D. (1974) (ed.) *Rousseau's Emile*, London: Routledge.

Jones, S. (1989) *Hazlitt: A Life*, Oxford: Oxford University Press.

Judt, T. (2004) Foreword to E.W. Said, *From Oslo to Iraq and the Roadmap*, London: Bloomsbury.

Karpf, A. (2006) 'Generation stressed', *Guardian*, *G2*, 13 September, p. 12–13.

Kitson, P.J. (1998) 'Beyond the Enlightenment: the philosophical, scientific and religious inheritance', in D. Wu (ed.), *A Companion to Romanticism*, Oxford: Basil Blackwell.

Kompridis, N. (2006) (ed.) *Philosophical Romanticism*, London: Routledge.

Liston, D. (2000) 'Love and despair in teaching', *Educational Theory*, 50.1: 81–102.

Liston, D. and Garrison, J. (eds) (2004) *Teaching, Learning and Loving: Reclaiming Passion in Educational Practice*, London: RoutledgeFalmer.

Lodge, C. (2003) Editorial, *Pastoral Care*, December, 3–4.

Lovejoy, A. (1924) 'On the discrimination of Romanticisms', *Publications of the Modern Language Association of America*, 39: 229–53.

Macarthur, E. (2003) *Taking on the World*, London: Penguin.

Maclean, C.M. (1943) *Born Under Saturn: A Biography of William Hazlitt*, London: Collins.

Mahoney, J.L. (1981) *The Logic of Passion: The Literary Criticism of William Hazlitt*, New York: Fordham University Press.

Maleuvre, D. (2005) 'Art and the teaching of love', *Journal of Aesthetics Education*, 39.1: 77–92.

Marai, S. (1942) *Embers*, trans. Carol Brown Janeway (repr. 2003), London: Penguin.

Marples, M. (1967) *Romantics at School*, London: Faber & Faber.

McCalman, I. (2001) Introduction, *An Oxford Companion to the Romantic Age*, Oxford: Oxford University Press.

McGann, J. (1983) *The Romantic Ideology: A Critical Investigation*, Chicago, IL: Chicago University Press.

McGavran, J.H. (1991) (ed.) *Romanticism and Children's Literature in Nineteenth-Century England*, Athens, GA: University of Georgia Press.

McIntyre, J. (1987) *Faith, Theology and Imagination*, Edinburgh: Handsel Press.

Mellor, A.K. (1988) (ed.) *Romanticism and Feminism*, Bloomington, IN: Indiana State University.

—— (1993) *Romanticism and Gender*, London: Routledge.

Mills, C.W. (1959) *The Sociological Imagination*, Oxford: Oxford University Press.

Moore, A. (2004) *The Good Teacher: Dominant Discourses in Teaching and Teacher Education*, London: RoutledgeFalmer.

Murdoch, I. (1969) *The Nice and the Good*, London: Chatto & Windus.

—— (1970) *The Sovereignty of Good*, London, Routledge & Kegan Paul.

Natarajan, U. (1998) *Hazlitt and the Reach of Sense: Criticism, Morals and the Metaphysics of Power*, Oxford: Clarendon Press.

Natarajan, U., Paulin, T. and Wu, D. (2005) (eds) *Metaphysical Hazlitt*, London: Routledge.

Park, R. (1971) *Hazlitt and the Spirit of the Age: Abstractionism and Critical Theory*, Oxford: Clarendon Press.

Paulin, T. (1998) *The Day-Star of Liberty: William Hazlitt's Radical Style*, London: Faber & Faber.

Perry, S. (1968) 'Romanticism: a brief history of a concept', in D. Wu (ed.), *A Companion to Romanticism*, Oxford: Basil Blackwell.

Peters, R.S. (1966) *Ethics and Education*, London: George Allen & Unwin.

—— (1973) *Reason and Compassion*, London: Routledge & Kegan Paul.

—— (1981) 'The paradoxes in Rousseau's *Emile*', in R.S. Peters (ed.), *Essays on Educators*, London: George Allen & Unwin.

Phillips, A. (2006) *Side Effects*, London: Hamish Hamilton.

Porter, R. (1982) *English Society in the Eighteenth Century*, Harmondsworth: Penguin.

Porter, R. and Teich, M. (eds) (1988) *Romanticism in National Context*, Cambridge: Cambridge University Press.

Postman, N. and Weingartner, C. (1971) *Teaching as a Subversive Activity*, Harmondsworth: Penguin.

Pring, R. (1984) *Personal and Social Education in the Curriculum*, London: Hodder & Stoughton.

Richards, I.A. (ed.) (1978) *The Portable Coleridge*, London: Penguin.

Richardson, A. (1994) *Literature, Education and Romanticism: Reading as Social Practice 1780–1832*, Cambridge: Cambridge University Press.

Rorty, R. (1982) 'Hermeneutics, general studies and teaching', *Synergos*, 2 (autumn): 1–15.

Rose, N. (1989) *Governing the Soul: The Shaping of the Private Self*, London: Routledge.

Rosenberg, A. (1990) 'Rousseau's *Emile*: the nature and purpose of education', in Willenski (ed.) 1990.

Ross, M. (1989) *The Contours of Masculine Desire: Romanticism and the Rise of Women's Poetry*, New York: Macmillan.

Rousseau, J.-J. (1762) *Emile*, in Jimack (ed.) 1974.

Said, E.W. (1994) *Representations of the Intellectual*, London: Vintage.

—— (2001a) 'On defiance and taking positions', in E. Said (ed.), *Reflections on Exile and Other Literary and Cultural Essays*, London: Granta.

—— (2001b) 'Remembrance of things played: presence and memory in the pianist's art', in E. Said (ed.), *Reflections on Exile and Other Literary and Cultural Essays*, London: Granta.

—— (2001c) 'Amateur of the insoluble', in E. Said (ed.), *Reflections on Exile and Other Literary and Cultural Essays*, London: Granta.

Schlipp, P.A. (1974) (ed.) *The Philosophy of Karl Popper* (Book1), Las Salle, Illinois: Open Court.

Schon, D.A. (1983) *The Reflective Practitioner*, New York: Basic Books.

Schwab, J.J. 1983) 'The practical 4: something for curriculum professors to do', *Curriculum Inquiry*, 13.3: 239–65.

Scruton, R. (1986) *Sexual Desire: A Philosophical Investigation*, London: Weidenfeld & Nicolson.

Sikes, H.M. (1978) (ed.) *The Letters of William Hazlitt*, London: Macmillan.

Simon, B. (1974) *The Two Nations and the Educational Structure, 1780–1870*, London: Lawrence & Wishart.

Simon, R.I. (1992) *Teaching against the Grain: Texts for a Pedagogy of Possibility*, New York: Bergin & Garvey.

Singer, I. (1966) *The Nature of Love: Plato to Luther*, Chicago, IL: University of Chicago Press.

—— (1984) *The Nature of Love: Courtly and Romantic*, Chicago, IL: University of Chicago Press.

Sisman, A. (2006) *The Friendship: Wordsworth and Coleridge*, London: Harper Press.

Steiner, G. (2003) *Lessons of the Masters*, Cambridge, MA: Harvard University Press.

Stenhouse, L. (1975) *An Introduction to Curriculum Research and Development*, London: Heinemann.

Stone, L. (1979) *The Family, Sex and Marriage in England, 1500–1800*, London: Weidenfeld & Nicolson.

Sutton-Smith, B. (1988) 'In search of the imagination', in K. Egan and D. Nadaner (eds), *Imagination and Education*, Milton Keynes: Open University Press.

Thompson, E.P. (1968) *The Making of the English Working Class*, Harmondsworth: Penguin.

Thurley, G. (1983) *The Romantic Predicament*, London: Macmillan.

Tillich, P. (1953) *Systematic Theology* (Vol. 1), London: Nisbet.

Todd, S. (2003) 'A fine risk to be run? The ambiguity of eros and teacher responsibility', *Studies in Philosophy and Education*, 22: 31–44.

Tomlinson, J. and Tomlinson, J. (2005) *The Luxury of Time*, London: Pocket Books.

UNICEF (2007) *An Overview of Child Well-Being in Rich Countries* (Report Card 7), Florence, Italy, Innocenti Research Centre.

Vernon, M. (2005) *The Philosophy of Friendship*, London: Palgrave.

Wardle, D. (1970) *English Popular Education 1870–1970*, Cambridge: Cambridge University Press.

Warnock, M. (1976) *Imagination*, London: Faber & Faber.

Wasserman, E.R. (1964) 'The English Romantics: the grounds of knowledge', *Studies in Romanticism*, 4: 14–32.

Whelan, M. (2003) *In the Company of William Hazlitt: Thoughts for the 21st Century*, London: Merlin Press.

Willensky, J. (ed.) (1990) *The Educational Legacy of Romanticism*, Ontario: Wilfrid Laurier.

Williams, R. (1961) *Culture and Society 1780–1950*, Harmondsworth: Penguin.

—— (1965) *The Long Revolution*, Harmondsworth: Penguin.

Williams, Z. (2006) *The Commercialisation of Childhood*, London: Compass.

Wilson, D.B. (1993) *The Romantic Dream*, Lincoln, NEB, and London: University of Nebraska Press.

Wordsworth, J. (1982) *William Wordsworth: The Borders of Vision*, Oxford: Clarendon Press.

Wordsworth, J. and Wordsworth, J. (eds) (2003) *The New Penguin Book of Romantic Poetry*, London: Penguin.

Wu, D. (ed.) (1998) *The Selected Writings of William Hazlitt*, London: Pickering & Chatto.

Wu, D. (2006) 'Hazlitt v. Coleridge', Second Annual Hazlitt Society Lecture, Conway Hall, London, 9 September.

Index

Blake, William
his conception of childhood   37–40

Childhood
and Blake, William   37–40, 47–8
'death' of   146–7
origins and significance   31–2
views of   33–6
and *Emile* (Rousseau, Jean-Jacques)
    36–7, 46–7
and Wordsworth, William   40–5, 47–8
and Dickens, Charles   34
and Locke, John   35

Coleridge, Samuel Taylor
critic of 'chalk & talk' teaching
    methods   2
commitment to the cause of popular
    education   2
marriage   12
character and achievements   27–8
final words on dying   29
his theoretical ideal of love   77–8
and German idealist philosophy
    108–9
his psychology of the imagination
    109, 111–13
his alleged political apostasy 138

Criticism
characteristics   143
and courage   140
and education academics   140, 142–3
and essay writing   140–2

and Hazlitt, William   134–6, 143
and honesty   137
and intellectuals   132–3, 136
and journalism   133
and literary style   141, 143
and Said, Edward   136
and steadfastness   136

Hazlitt, William
character   25–7
at New College, Hackney   56–61, 83
first meeting with Coleridge,
    Samuel T   136f
final breach with Coleridge,
    Samuel T   137–9
self-portrait   24f
gravestone   27
infatuated with Sarah Walker (*Liber
    Amoris*)   73
John Clare's impressions   25
final words on dying   29
views about a real education   60
views about the value of commonsense
    121
attitudes towards a classical education
    61
ambivalence about the need for a
    national system of education   60
on the importance of reading   68
and *gusto*   88
on writing poetry   88
his theory of sympathetic and
    disinterested benevolence   117–20
his attack on 'Mr Gifford'   122

on consistency of argument   129
his intellectualism   135f
similarities with Edward Said   136
his prose style (after Tom Paulin) 141–3

Heroism
characteristics   95
and confidence   94–5
and hero-worship   95
and inspiration   96
and motivation   96
and Napoleon   93–4
and optimism   102
and revolution   93–4
and Romantic poetry   92–3
and school leaders   100–3
and teachers   99–100
and Egan, Kieran   94–5

Imagination
and agency   105–6, 111, 124
and 'becoming'   114
and the Bible   106
and classical education   61–2
and Coleridge, Samuel T   109–13
and the Good   106–7
and happiness   111
and Hazlitt, William   117–20
and images   115–16
and joy   109–10
and Nature   63–5
and 'negative education'   67
and reading   60, 65, 68
and recollection   114–15, 126
and restoration   115–16, 126
and sympathy   117–18, 125
and teaching   122–4
and the Truth   107
and usurpation   110–25
and Wordsworth, William   114–17

Love
and actualization   79
agape   75, 76
characteristics   74–7

and Coleridge, Samuel T   77–8
elusiveness of   80–1
eros   75
and friendship   77, 84
and the Good   86, 87, 90
and *gusto*   88
and Hazlitt, William   73
and identity   79
and mutual separateness   84
and passion   86–90
and pedagogy   81–6
philia   74, 75–6, 82
and sympathy   78
and teaching   86

Progressive education
characteristics   9–10
and personhood   17–18
and democracy   17
links with Romanticism 22–3

Romanticism
characteristics of   15, 18–20, 22–3,
   28–9
and displacing ideal   20
and dreaming   15–16
and energy   23
and the Enlightenment   20–1
and feminism   12–13
and *Hope and Education*   14
and power   23
and progressive education   3–5, 9–10
and Romance   11
and the Romantic character   24–9
and utopianism   14–15

Rousseau, Jean-Jacques
and a 'negative education'   67
and time wasting   48
Emile   36–7, 45–7
and Wordsworth, William   44–5

Wordsworth, William
his support for the 'Madras System'
   48f

and *Emile* 44–5
commitment to the cause of popular
  education 2
his criticism of transmitting facts 2
his conception of childhood 40–3

at Hawkshead Grammar School
  61–6
and book learning 65, 68
and learning from Nature 65
his theory of the imagination 114–17